Learning Through Children's Eyes

PSYCHOLOGY IN THE CLASSROOM: A SERIES ON APPLIED EDUCATIONAL PSYCHOLOGY

A collaborative project of APA Division 15 (Educational Psychology) and APA Books.

Barbara L. McCombs and Sharon McNeely, Series Editors

Advisory Board

Series Titles

Becoming Relfective Students and Teachers With Portfolios and Authentic Assessment—Paris & Ayres

Creating Culturally Responsive Classrooms—Shade, Kelly, & Oberg

Creating Responsible Learners: The Role of a Positive Classroom Environment—Ridley & Walther

Developing Self-Regulated Learners: Beyond Achievement to Self-Efficacy—Zimmerman, Boner, & Kovach

Inventive Strategies for Teaching Mathematics—Middleton & Goepfert

Motivating Hard to Reach Students—McCombs & Pope

New Approaches to Literacy: Helping Students Develop Reading and Writing Skills—Marzano & Paynter

Overcoming Student Failure: Changing Motives and Incentives for Learning—Covington & Teel

Real-Life Problem Solving: A Collaborative Approach to Interdisciplinary Learning—Jones, Rasmussen & Moffitt

Study Strategies for Lifelong Learning—Weinstein & Hume

Teaching for Thinking—Sternberg & Spear-Swerling

Learning Through Children's Eyes
Social Constructivism and the Desire to Learn

Penny Oldfather and Jane West
with
Jennifer White and Jill Wilmarth

American Psychological Association | Washington, DC

First Printing, June 1999
Second Printing, September 2000
Third Printing, October 2003
Published by
American Psychological Association
750 First Street, NE
Washington, DC 20002

Copies may be ordered from
APA Order Department
P.O. Box 92984
Washington, DC 20090-2984

In the UK and Europe, copies may be ordered from
American Psychological Association
3 Henrietta Street
Covent Garden, London
WC2E 8LU England

Typeset in Berkeley and Bell Gothic by Monotype Composition, Baltimore, MD
Printer: Sheridan Books, Inc., Fredericksburg, VA
Cover Designer: Minker Design, Bethesda, MD
Technical/Production Editor: Eleanor Inskip

Library of Congress Cataloging-in-Publication Data
Oldfather, Penny.
    Learning through children's eyes : social constructivism and the
    desire to learn / Penny Oldfather and Jane West with Jennifer White
    and Jill Wilmarth.
        p.   cm. — (Psychology in the classroom)
    Includes bibliographical references.
    ISBN 1-55798-587-1 (ppk. : alk. paper)
    1. Learning, Psychology of.   2. Motivation in education.
3. Cognition in children.   4. Social interaction in children.
5. Constructivism (Education)   I. West, Jane, 1960–   .   II. Title.
III. Series.
LB1060.043   1999
370.15'23—dc21   99-12929
                                                              CIP

British Library Cataloguing-in-Publication Data
A CIP record is available from the British Library.

Printed in the United States of America

CONTENTS

PREFACE

What does it mean to look at learning through children's eyes?

> [Our teacher] lets us participate and she lets us tell the answers. She doesn't tell all the answers. She knows that she's not perfect. . . . She has to hear it from other people that they understand.
>
> Lauren, fifth grader

> Miss Rice decided to have workshops so everyone could do fun activities instead of doing work. . . . I didn't really like it the way it used to be. All you did was work. Now, you can pick whichever thing you want to, work with different people, pick your books. Everybody likes it. You get to write about things you want to write about.
>
> Kendra, third grader

Lauren recognizes the ways that her teacher's decisions are grounded in the children's perspectives. Kendra is experiencing a newfound freedom to learn, which she attributes to her teacher's purposeful decision "to have workshops" as part of a restructured curriculum. This book illustrates the ways that teachers, by seeing learning through children's eyes, create new possibilities for their students' intrinsic motivation and meaningful learning. Motivation and learning are linked in a view of knowledge that is called *social constructivism*, the theory that undergirds the ideas in this book.

Social constructivist theorists acknowledge multiple constructions of the world. In social constructivist theory, each human being makes sense of the world in a unique way. For teachers to facilitate students' learning, therefore, it is essential that they seek to understand students' unique constructions and to see learning through their students' eyes. Social constructivism has major implications for the ways we understand learning, the ways we as teachers think about our roles, and the ways we teach.

Our main purpose in this book is to propose a vision of the ways that learning experiences are transformed when teachers see learning through children's eyes. Educators, parents, and students alike agree that intrinsically motivated, meaningful learning is not the primary experience of many students in schools (Cross, 1990; O'Flahavan et al., 1992). Prevalent educational practices often disrupt students' natural yearnings to understand their worlds (Kohn, 1993). Many students experience school as someone else's agenda, as a place where they feel invisible. This may be particularly the case for students with culturally and linguistically diverse backgrounds (Lampkins, 1997; Perry, 1997; Willis, 1987). In such environments, teachers may lose opportunities to "get into students' heads" and to support their sense-making effectively. These teaching opportunities can be rediscovered when teachers seek children's perspectives. Seeing learning through children's eyes brings about important changes in classroom culture, including changing ways that curriculum is negotiated and enacted, changing the content of the curriculum, and changing relationships among all members of the classroom community. These changes, in turn, add a joyful dimension that is clearly evident in the children's classroom experiences described in this book. Readers will note that we have used the plural form, understandings, throughout the book. We choose this unconventional form intentionally, in order to emphasize the social constructivist principle of multiple constructions of reality.

When teachers and students reflect and talk openly about what helps their motivation and learning, they have better access to both their own and each other's perspectives. We believe that seeking, respecting, and understanding children's viewpoints as learners and knowers must be the basis for both long-term and moment-to-moment decision making in classrooms. Regardless of whether your students are four years old or forty, whether they are learning about tadpoles or about Piaget, we hope that you will find this book a helpful resource and a catalyst for your thinking about teaching and learning.

This work "stands on the shoulders" of other researchers—including motivation theorists, literacy researchers, constructivist theorists, and researchers of sociocultural issues—who have explored contexts supporting meaningful learning. (See the suggested readings at the end of each goal.) This book builds upon their work in several ways:

1. By making theoretical links between children's knowledge construction and intrinsic motivations for learning.

2. By examining those links from our perspectives as classroom teacher and school administrator, preservice teacher, and two university-based teacher educators, and through the eyes of many children from a wide range of grade levels.

3. By offering strategies through which teachers can access their students' perspectives.

One strategy is the Children's Thinking Project (Oldfather, Bonds, & Bray, 1994), which we describe in detail in Goal 2. A second strategy is the use of children's and adolescents' literature to explore issues of social constructivism.

Among the titles mentioned here, you will find references to old favorites and some new selections. These books can be used as springboards for discussion between adults and children about what promotes learning and motivation.

In keeping with the principles of social constructivism, we have designed this book in a way that requires the readers' active participation. Many of the concepts are most easily understood through experience and reflection. You will gain the most if you engage in the processes that are suggested throughout the text, such as the children's thinking project, literature discussions, autobiographical exploration, classroom evaluation, and self-directed questions.

Our work together has enabled us to further our understandings of social constructivism by seeing the issues and possibilities through each other's eyes. Jill is a beginning teacher and recent graduate in education and religious studies at Agnes Scott College. Jennifer, currently a school administrator, was an elementary school teacher when we began this project. Jane, a former middle school teacher, is now an assistant professor in the teacher education program at Agnes Scott College. Penny has been involved in public education from kindergarten through high school and is currently an associate professor at The University of Georgia. The four of us grappled with the meanings of social constructivism from our various perspectives as we spent time in Jennifer's classroom, and as we read and discussed professional literature and children's books related to these issues.

ACKNOWLEDGMENTS

We are indebted to our families for supporting our work and taking up the slack when we were busy writing. We also want to thank our editors, Barbara McCombs and Sharon McNeely, for their expert guidance and also Adrian Harris Forman for her very thoughtful review of our manuscript. We appreciate the hospitality of the Great American Steak House and Buffet Company, which opened early for us for several Saturday morning work sessions. Finally, our greatest debt is to all the students who have been in our classrooms and who have participated in our research. Among them are people you will "meet" in this book: Abby Potts, Mariposa Arillo, Debbie Davis, Joy Garwood, Christopher Hayes, Alicia Lindsey, Amanda Lockhart, Kathleen Mazurek, Cyndy Piha, Olivia Roller, Jennifer Woodruff, and Akpene Zikpi. Many of the ideas expressed in this book came from our experiences with them. We have learned most of all through their eyes.

Introduction

A Morning in
Jennifer's Classroom

Come with us to Jennifer's kindergarten classroom and watch as students take charge of their own learning during reading workshop on this spring morning. Their chosen books in hand, children select their favorite reading spots, some at tables, some on the carpet, others in the reading area or in chairs they have pulled to the center of the room. Remembering yesterday's trip to a strawberry farm, two girls cuddle in the big rocking chair, reading *The Little Mouse, the Red Ripe Strawberry, and the Big Hungry Bear* (Wood & Wood, 1984). Several others stand together at the front of the room, reading to an imaginary audience in the expressive style Jennifer uses when she reads to them. Other children cluster around a big book version of *Rosie's Walk* (Hutchins, 1968), poring over the pictures and text. Jennifer moves from child to child, listening to them read, talking with them, and posing questions about their books.

"It's time to find a stopping place and come sit on the rug," Jennifer announces after about 30 minutes. The children begin to close their books and gather for sharing time, the final phase of their workshop. Jennifer asks for volunteers to read to the class. Hands shoot into the air. Consulting her record chart, Jennifer calls on a student who has not recently read to the class. Each of the three students who takes the seat labeled "author's chair" reads into the hand-held mike and invites comments from classmates.

Abby is the last one called on to share. As depicted on the cover of this book, she takes three books with her to the author's chair, sits down, crosses her legs primly, and takes up the microphone. We smile as we watch her hold up each book in turn, reading the title and author, and announcing, "You get to vote on which book you want me to read." Returning to the first book, she asks, "Who wants this one?" Several students raise their hands. She repeats this procedure with the second and third books, pointing to each raised hand as she counts the votes aloud and then announcing the tally each time. Jennifer, who is seated in a child-size chair near the back of the group, observes this spontaneous "teacherly" survey with interest, raising her hand along with the children to cast her vote. Upon hearing the winning title, several children whisper, "Yes!" and pump their arms in celebration. Abby reads the entire story, panning the book from left to right as she shows each picture so that all her classmates can see. She conducts class confidently as if this were a daily event for her.

At the conclusion of the story, Abby issues the customary call for "questions or comments" about her reading. Several hands go up, and she calls on Curtis, who is eager to participate, despite the difficulties he often experiences in literacy learning. He remarks, "I think you're doing a very good job reading. Why did you choose those three books?"

Holding up each book in turn, she explains, "I chose *this* one because I practiced it at home and I knew I could read it. And I chose *this* one because it was scary and I thought people would like it. And *this* one I practiced, and no one has ever shared it with the class before. I thought you might enjoy hearing it." Discussion over, Abby returns to her seat on the carpet.

CONSIDERING WHAT WE HAVE SEEN

What enables these kindergarten children to use literacy in such personally meaningful, interactive ways? What roles do voice and choice play in this community? What enables Abby to feel comfortable initiating such an enterprise with such poise, and to offer her classmates choices through this highly structured, teacherlike survey? What enables Curtis as a struggling learner to construct a question of such quality and depth, to compliment Abby so generously, and to feel confident about his own public participation in literacy events?

What does it mean that Jennifer sits in the back and participates in the survey as any other member of the class might do? What can we learn by taking note of the shared spaces in this classroom, such as the adult-sized rocking chair and the author's chair at the front of the room? Why is the teacher's desk tucked out of the way in the back and used only for storage, while Jennifer shares the other spaces in the room (including the tiny chairs and tables) with the children? The answers to these questions lie within Jennifer's philosophy of social constructivism, which is reflected in the culture of her classroom. As the remainder of this book unfolds, we will return to these issues of classroom relationships.

A QUICKWRITE ON CLASSROOM CULTURE

Select a few of the questions posed in the previous paragraph as topics and quickwrite for 5 minutes to clarify your ideas. What elements of the culture of Jennifer's classroom do you find most striking? Spend a few minutes thinking about the issues involved, write your thoughts in the space provided below, and discuss them with your colleagues..

OVERVIEW OF THE BOOK

We hope our description of Jennifer's classroom prompts you to consider your teaching practices. Whatever your current situation—whether you are a teacher reading on your own, a student in a teacher education course, or a teacher in a professional development course or after-school study group. This book will provide several tools to stimulate thinking. Vignettes from real classrooms, questions for consideration and discussion, and specific strategies for accessing children's thinking are some of the strategies employed. We also incorporate many children's books and literature discussion strategies. We suggest questions that readers might use in exploring essential characteristics of meaningful learning. Additional resources include professional readings, an annotated bibliography of children's books, and a glossary.

STATEMENT OF GOALS

This book is organized by four learning goals to assist you in understanding social constructivism:

1. Understanding social constructivism as a basis for meaningful learning and intrinsic motivation.

2. Accessing students' thinking and deepening understandings of social constructivism.

3. Envisioning classroom practices that flow from a social constructivist stance.

4. Considering possibilities and challenges of seeing learning through children's eyes.

Goal 1

Understanding Social Constructivism as a Basis for Meaningful Learning and Intrinsic Motivation

Cyndy: Where do you think artists get their ideas?

Eli: From their head.

Cyndy: How do they get in their head?

Eli: From their mind.

Cyndy: Yea, but how does it get there, where does it come from to get into their mind?

Eli: God.

Cyndy: Oh, God puts it there. That's an interesting idea. I wonder where God gets the ideas.

Eli: He sends them down into the person who's thinking about something and it goes into his head and then he has an idea.

Cyndy: And then what does he do with that idea?

Eli: He draws it on a piece of paper!

[Excerpt from a taped conversation for a Children's Thinking Project conducted by Cyndy Piha with her son, Eli]

Theory matters. We all have theories, whether we are conscious of them or not. Our theories about what constitutes knowledge, what it means to "know," and how we come to know have a major impact on the ways that we teach and on the ways that students experience learning. Although they sometimes go unexamined or unrecognized, theories have a profound influence on the ways we conceptualize our roles, interact with students, develop and enact curriculum, and organize classrooms. Much educational research (e.g., Dyson, 1989, 1991; Dahl & Freppon, 1995; Oldfather & Dahl, 1994) supports social constructivism as a theory of knowledge that enables teachers to promote their students' meaningful learning and intrinsic motivation. Taking a social constructivist stance leads teachers to see learning through children's eyes, and therefore, to become more responsive teachers. In this goal we will examine social constructivism: define the theory and explain its relevance for learning and intrinsic motivation.

> Theories have a profound influence on the ways we conceptualize our roles, interact with students, develop and enact curriculum, and organize classrooms.

WHAT IS SOCIAL CONSTRUCTIVISM?

Social constructivism is a particular view of knowledge, a view of how we come to know. In this view, learning is constructed through interactions with others, which take place within a specific socio-cultural context. A social constructivist perspective focuses on learning as sense-making rather than on the acquisition of role knowledge that "exists" somewhere outside the learner. Piaget (1955) viewed learning as invention; teachers see this process take place in their classrooms every day as their students are involved in "the having of wonderful ideas" (Duckworth, 1987).

> A social constructivist perspective focuses on learning as sense-making rather than on the acquisition of rote knowledge that "exists" somewhere outside the learner.

Piaget's theories focus primarilyon individuals' constructions (Wood, Bruner, & Ross, 1976), Vygotsky's (1978) emphasize the inherently social nature of learning. Vygotsky's observations about the relation between thought and language have significantly expanded views of learning. The relations can be seen in this way:

We Acquire and Use Language Socially

Babies learn to understand and use language within a social context (usually within their families). Our earliest language is primarily external. For example, you may have observed a young child narrating while drawing a picture or instructing aloud while building a block tower. An emergent reader will need to read aloud and may have difficulty reading silently. After becoming a more proficient language user, the child internalizes speech and no longer needs to verbalize.

The particular culture of the family influences the child's use and understanding of language. For example, Heath (1983) studied language and literacy practices in three southern mountain communities. She found that in some subcultures, families asked questions for which they knew the answers as a means of "instructing" or teaching their children about the world. For example, a parent might point to a tree and ask the child, "What's that?" In other subcultures, parents asked their children questions only to elicit information that they, the parents did not already have (e.g., "Where is your sister?"). When children in the latter group went to school, they encountered questions that were used instructionally from teachers (e.g., "What's the capital of our state?"). This created difficulty for some children who had constructed a different understanding of the intentions behind questions. It also created misunderstandings on the part of teachers about what the children did or did not understand. The socio-cultural roots of language must be taken into account as educators attempt to facilitate students' learning.

Language Is the Basis for Thought

Our capacity for thought is developed primarily through our acquisition of language. Language enables us to name the world and our experiences within it, to differentiate ourselves from the world, and to find our place in it. Through language (and other socially derived signs or tools, such as musical and mathematical notation), we manipulate concepts, understand relationships, and organize ideas: We develop abilities for abstraction. For example, students studying the solar system develop concepts about the nature of planets, moons, and stars: their components, their enormous scale, their movements in relation to each other, and how human beings fit into this large picture. Language is the primary medium through which this learning occurs. The concepts that are developed lay a foundation upon which the students can build an increasingly complex understanding of the universe and their place in it. What a wonder it is that language empowers us to ponder the origins of the universe!

Language can constrain or expand knowledge constructions (Kelly & Green, 1998; Strike & Posner, 1992). For example, the Inuit people have many different words for *snow*. This highly differentiated language facilitates the Inuk child's thinking about snow in complex ways. In contrast, a child in the southwest, who has more limited experience with snow and who is exposed to only one word for snow, would be likely to have a simpler, less sophisticated way of perceiving snow. According to Wardhaugh (1990),

> if one language makes distinctions that another does not make, then those who use the first language will more readily perceive the differences in their environment which such linguistic distinctions draw attention to. If you must classify snow, camels, and automobiles in certain ways, you will perceive snow, camels, and automobiles differently from someone who is not required to make these differentiations. (p. 214)

In sum, the language we use shapes and is shaped by our membership within families and communities.

Therefore, Sense-making, Learning, Has Socio-cultural Roots

Language is entwined with thought and thus lies at the heart of our sense-making about the world. As our inner thoughts are rooted in language, they are inherently social, like language.

These fundamental premises of social constructivism have important implications for pedagogy and for daily life in classrooms. They call for us as educators to look deeply into issues regarding diverse languages and cultures of our society. These principles require careful consideration of the significance of language for our children, not only for their academic learning, but also for their self-esteem and identity development.

The debate surrounding Ebonics is a case in point. *Ebonics* (which literally means "Black sounds") is a term used by linguists who have traced the historical roots and structures of language spoken by African Americans to the West and Niger–Congo languages of Africa. In a 1997 resolution, the Linguistic Society of America (LSA) took the position that whether one chooses to call it Ebonics, African American Vernacular English (AAVE) or Vernacular Black English, this language is "systematic and rule-governed like all natural speech varieties. . . . Characterizations of Ebonics as 'slang,' 'mutant,' 'lazy,' 'ineffective,' 'ungrammatical,' or 'broken English' are incorrect and demeaning" (p. 27).

Thus, Ebonics issues concern both pedagogy and self-esteem and identity. Consider what it means to children who are told by well-meaning teachers when they go to school that there is something inherently "wrong" with the way of speaking of their people. Lisa Delpit (1997) wrote:

> I have been asked often enough recently, "What do you think about Ebonics? Are you for it or against it?" My answer must be neither. I can be neither for Ebonics or against Ebonics any more than I can be for or against air. It exists. It is the language spoken by many of our African-American children. It is the language they heard as their mothers nursed them and changed their diapers and played peek-a-boo with them. It is the language through which they first encountered love, nurturance, and joy. (p. 6)

Events that occurred in Oakland, California during the mid 1990s highlight the importance of taking into account Black students' language (and culture) in developing effective pedagogy. The overall grade point average in the Oakland school district was 2.4. For White students, it was 2.7; for Black students, 1.8. However, in one particular Oakland school, African American students had above-average GPAs. In that school, most of the teachers had participated in a research-based initiative called Standard English Proficiency Program (SEP). Through SEP they had learned about Ebonics or AAVE language patterns so that they could "build on the history, culture and language of African American students" and thereby help students "build a bridge to Standard English" (Getridge, 1997, p. 27). The remarkable effectiveness of that program led the Oakland school board to require all schools to participate in SEP—a decision that set off a rancorous debate that received national attention. (See Related Readings at the end of Goal 1 for further information.)

The hot debate surrounding the Ebonics issue in Oakland exemplifies ways that issues of language, culture, and power play out within public schools. This debate also illustrates that a holistic view of social constructivism must take into account students' languages and cultures. Educators are then forced to acknowledge that their work extends into the political realm. To their students, teachers represent authority concerning what counts for knowledge and whose knowledge counts. When teachers fail to acknowledge students' worlds the students are likely to feel alienated or even invisible.

CLASSROOM CULTURE AND SOCIAL CONSTRUCTIVISM

Social constructivism stretches us to think beyond narrow, curricular goals and to reach toward broad purposes of learning such as students' self-knowledge, development of identities, and belief that they can make a difference in the world. For example, when Abby conducted her book survey in Jennifer's classroom (see p. 2), she was doing much more than simply demonstrating her progress in reading. She was also constructing a sense of herself as reader, literary critic, lover of books, class leader, facilitator of democratic processes, and initiator of action. A social constructivist understanding of this event recognizes that Abby's development in reading was connected to the *whole* of her understanding, experiences, roles, and sense of self. A social constructivist view of this event also helps us see the role of classroom culture in Abby's actions.

SELF-DIRECTED QUESTION

1 What kind of learning environment made it possible for Abby to select books to share, conduct a survey of preferences, employ a democratic process for her survey, invite questions, and overlook the teacher's raised hand?

Here is what we noticed about Jennifer's classroom as we thought about Abby's experience:

☐ Traditional student and teacher roles were viewed flexibly. Jennifer became a student, Abby became a teacher, and the other students accepted the reversed roles without question.

☐ Learners were understood to be question posers and decision makers who could take the initiative, participate in shaping curriculum, think carefully about the purposes of learning, and have a say in what happens.

☐ Curriculum was often negotiated among all members of the group and many decisions were made democratically; student choice was valued and supported.

☐ Members of the class were a kind of "family." They supported each other's learning and celebrated each other's successes. They felt safe to participate without fear of ridicule.

☐ The self-confidence demonstrated by both Curtis and Abby illustrates Jennifer's underlying faith that *everybody* can experience success.

☐ In whole–group meetings, hands were raised, and people were called on for turn taking. Students listened and responded to each other without constant teacher direction to do so.

☐ The position in the front of the classroom that traditionally belongs to teachers was a shared space.

☐ Everyone understood how "author's chair" worked. A ritual had been established, and the children knew what to expect.

☐ The teacher shared the "ownership of knowing," that is, she did not position herself as the sole source of knowledge. Abby's carefully considered rationales for the books she had chosen, and her poise and confidence suggested that she knew that her knowledge counted and that Jennifer and the children respected her ideas.

These aspects of Jennifer's classroom reflect the culture of the classroom. *Classroom culture* is a set of *taken-as-shared* (Cobb, Yackel, & Wood, 1992) understandings regarding roles, rules, relationships, and notions of authority. "At most, cultural knowledge can be only assumed, or 'taken-as-shared,' by its members. Yet cultural knowledge is a whole that is larger than the sum of individual cognitions" (Fosnot, 1996, p. 24). These understandings, which permeate classroom life, are socially constructed by the participants.

You can probably tell a few things about the culture of a classroom when you enter. Whether the environment is welcoming or threatening, teacher-dominated or student-centered, joyful or stressful is often immediately evident to a classroom visitor. From your own experience as a student, you may remember substitute teachers who didn't do things "right." They were outsiders to the culture of your classroom and did not know the "rules" about how things were done. Their lack of knowledge about the culture changed the way people felt about being in the classroom.

ACTIVITY

First Grade Takes a Test (Cohen, 1980) presents food for thought about what it means to "break the rules" of classroom culture. The first graders in this story experience quite a shift in the way they feel about themselves and their classroom environment when they are introduced to standardized testing. We encourage you to read this delightful little book and consider the following questions concerning its implications:

1. How does students' experience in taking the test go against the ways the children and teacher understand what it means to know something?

2. What are various explanations for why Anna Maria found the test questions easy to answer?

3. How does the children's experience in this classroom illustrate the ways that classroom culture is socially constructed?

Teachers are the keys to the establishment and maintenance of classroom culture. Their theories, beliefs, and values have a great effect on the kind of culture established. Students also have an impact in shaping the classroom culture. The ways in which they interact with each other and with the teacher (West, 1996b), the forms of leadership they assume, the goals they pursue, and the humor they inject, all come into play as the classroom participants interact to construct classroom culture. Jennifer's stance as a social constructivist, and her goals for her classroom of collaborative construction of meaning are evident in the interactions that take place in her classroom. She realizes the importance of thinking not only about teaching individual children, but also about being aware of the impact of the evolving classroom culture on students' learning and motivation. Through social interactions within the culture of a classroom, students construct (a) a sense of themselves as either capable or not-so-capable learners and knowers, (b) positive or negative attitudes toward learning, and (c) a sense of optimism and agency or of despair and helplessness.

SOCIAL CONSTRUCTIVISM AND MOTIVATION

Taking a social constructivist stance can enable teachers to create classrooms in which students can become intrinsically motivated to learn (Oldfather, 1993; Oldfather & Dahl, 1994; Oldfather & McLaughlin, 1993; Oldfather & Thomas, 1998; Oldfather & Thomas, in press; Short & Burke, 1991; Thomas & Oldfather, 1997). The form of intrinsic motivation that we have explored in our research is what Oldfather (1992) called *continuing impulse to learn* (CIL), which is defined as

> an on-going engagement in learning that is propelled and focused by thought and feeling emerging from the learners' processes of constructing meaning. The continuing impulse to learn is characterized by intense involvement, curiosity, and a search for understanding as learners experience learning as a deeply personal and continuing agenda. (p. 8)

This form of motivation is linked explicitly to learners' social construction of meaning. Instead of searching for ways to coerce students into learning what someone else has prescribed, social constructivist teachers are likely to focus their efforts on helping their students "find their passions, discover what they care about, create their own learning agendas, and most importantly, *connect who they are to what they do in school*" (Oldfather, 1992). Meaningful connections between learners' identities and school can foster lifelong learning and the development of important skills (McCombs, 1991; McCombs & Marzano, 1990).

Creating classrooms that foster the continuing impulse to learn begins with seeing learning through children's eyes. A social constructivist teacher knows that what children understand now determines what they can learn next. An awareness of students' understanding provides the information teachers need to scaffold or provide temporary support for, their students' learning and motivation (Wood, Bruner, & Ross, 1976).

> Social constructivist teachers are likely to focus their efforts on helping their students "find their passions, discover what they care about, create their own learning agendas, and most importantly, *connect who they are to what they do in school*."

Social constructivist teachers take into account the role of classroom culture in supporting students' intrinsic motivation. Such teachers can deliberately create classroom environments that are responsive to the needs, ideas, dreams, and feelings of their students. They involve students in the construction of curriculum (Nicholls & Hazzard, 1993). They also support a range of interests and learning styles by providing ample opportunity for social interaction and self-expression through a variety of media. Our colleague Sally Thomas described the culture she worked to establish in her fifth- and sixth-grade classroom as having a "rich broth of meaning" (Oldfather, 1993, p. 676). Ingredients in this "broth" of ideas come from a wide array of books, interesting people, and projects; discussions of current events; trips to the local theater; and attendance at a Ray Bradbury talk, to name a few examples.

Social constructivist teachers help their students understand that they are co-constructors of knowledge, that they can make sense of things themselves, and that they have the power to seek knowledge and to attempt to understand the world. Teachers who respect multiple constructions in this way are "sharing the ownership of knowing" (Oldfather & Dahl, 1994, p. 145) with their students, who gain a sense of their own intellectual agency. That is, students develop a sense of their active roles as producers—not only consumers—of knowledge. They perceive themselves as competent knowers and learners. When students feel that they can succeed or that challenging enterprises will make them better at something, they feel a sense of self-worth (Covington, 1985), and they are more likely to become engaged in learning (Deci & Ryan, 1987).

A classroom culture exemplifying these qualities supports students' intrinsic motivations. To be intrinsically engaged in learning, students need to experience a certain degree of autonomy or self-determination (Deci & Ryan, 1990). Students do not need or want to be self-determining in *everything*. If they have choices within some structures, however, these choices will go a long way toward enhancing their ownership of their learning.

Does this mean that in a social constructivist classroom anything goes? Not at all. Does the teacher provide students with more information if they have misconceptions? Of course. Often, however, the teacher does not simply "tell" the right answer immediately. Instead, the teacher takes an active role in scaffolding students' understanding to new levels, challenging them to think through their ideas by presenting them with contradictory evidence, asking them to show evidence and consider alternatives. But within this process, the emphasis is on understanding, on learning from mistakes. The integrity of each individual's learning process is respected. Does this mean that social constructivist teachers would have lower standards of quality? To the contrary. In our view, by focusing on in-depth understanding, the quality of learning is greatly enhanced. Teachers are more likely to see what students *do* know and understand, and consequently, to have higher expectations.

> Social constructivist teachers help their students understand that they are co-constructors of knowledge, that they can make sense of things themselves, and that they have the power to seek knowledge and to attempt to understand the world.

Enterprises that promote learners' intrinsic motivation are at the optimal challenge level, neither so easy that they seem purposeless nor so difficult that they seem impossible (Csikszentmihalyi, 1978). Many social constructivist teachers find ways to structure classroom activities so that they can often function as a "guide on the side," rather than a "sage on the stage" (Taylor, 1982). Learning is a collaborative enterprise in which students help each other (West, 1996b). We saw this kind of structure in Jennifer's classroom. As demonstrated in the following vignette, Jennifer's students were able to choose activities that were likely to be at their own optimal challenge level.

During center time in Jennifer's kindergarten classroom, when children were free to choose from among numerous pursuits, we saw Allison take the globe to her table and begin examining it carefully. After a few minutes, she went to the writing center, retrieved pencil and paper, and made a complete list of the continents. Noticing Allison's project, Jennifer approached and asked, "What's going on?" Allison explained what she was doing, and Jennifer replied, "Neat! Why don't you put them in alphabetical order now?" Clearly enjoying the challenge, Allison began working. "More than one of these starts with 'A,'" Jennifer pointed out. "When words start with the same letter, you have to look over at the second letter and see which of them comes first." Allison did not answer, but methodically and correctly alphabetized the continents, checking off each one from her original list as she went. When she was done, Allison took her list around the room, proudly displaying it to her classmates and several adults who were there, explaining what she had done. Jennifer's interaction with Allison built on Allison's self-initiated activity and scaffolded her thinking to a higher level.

THE SOCIAL CONSTRUCTIVIST CHALLENGE TO BEHAVIORIST THINKING

Shifting to a social constructivist stance requires us to reexamine behaviorist traditions that are often invisible but remain pervasive within the culture of schooling in the United States (Marshall, 1992). These traditions emphasize the effects of rewards and punishments and learned associations and behaviors. They stress practice on skills and focus on external motivations.

The roots of the behaviorist legacy can be traced to those pioneers such as John B. Watson (known as the father of behaviorism), and B. F. Skinner (and his work with operant conditioning). Behaviorism further penetrated the field of education through the pervasive influence of psychologist Edward Thorndike at Teachers College, Columbia, NY. Thorndike's behaviorist theories had an enormous influence on many teachers and educational leaders who attended that institution. Marshall (citing Farnham-Diggory) pointed out that "by 1940, nearly one-tenth of the teachers, more than one-half of big-city superintendents, and nearly one-third of the deans of colleges of education in the United States had attended Teachers College" (1992, p. 8).

How do social constructivists view behaviorist principles? Generally, social constructivists would not deny the short-term effectiveness of extrinsic rewards and punishments in getting students to do things. Nor would they deny the existence of learned associations. Most social constructivists, however, would argue that a behaviorist view of learning does not adequately take into account the role of learners' thinking, feelings, and intentions, or of the learners' goals and conceptual structures. Skinnerian behaviorists do not see intrinsic motivations as relevant to who we are as human beings. They see freedom as an illusion. They believe there is no such thing as a *self*.

Kohn (1993) describes B. F. Skinner's assumptions about humans in the following excerpt:

> [Skinner] insisted that organisms (including us, remember) are nothing more than "repertoires of behaviors," and these behaviors can be fully explained by outside forces he called "environmental contingencies." "A person is not an originat-

ing agent: he is a locus, a point at which many genetic and environmental conditions come together in a joint effect" (Skinner, 1974, p. 168). But this would seem to imply that there is no "self" as we usually use the term, would it not? Yes, indeed, replied Skinner. (p. 6)

The epilogue to Skinner's memoirs bears this out:

> I am sometimes asked, "Do you think of yourself as you think of the organisms you study?" The answer is yes. So far as I know, my behavior at any given moment has been nothing more than the product of my genetic endowment, my personal history, and the current setting. . . . If I am right about human behavior, I have written the autobiography of a nonperson. (cited in Kohn, 1993, p. 7)

This view of human nature is not one with which most educators would agree. It is, however, one of the hidden assumptions underlying widely used practices in classrooms: the indiscriminate administration of extrinsic rewards for learning. We will better fulfill our roles in educating citizens for a democratic society by helping students become responsible decision makers and critical thinkers, rather than by "training" them to respond to control by others.

Ironically, the reliance on extrinsic rewards can often backfire. Teachers with the best intentions unknowingly undermine students' intrinsic motivations. For example, by providing rewards (such as pizza) for reading a certain number of books, teachers may persuade students to read more books. However, children who have previously been rewarded by the pleasures of a good book may divert their attention away from these intrinsic motivations and focus instead on the extrinsic reward (Csikszentmihalyi, 1978). If those rewards are then removed, little of the original intrinsic motivation may remain. John Nicholls commented in Kohn (1993) that when we give children pizza in exchange for reading, we are in danger of ending up with "a lot of fat kids who don't like to read" (p. 73). From a social constructivist standpoint, of course, the readers in a food-for-reading program *are* constructing meaning, but consider what that meaning might be:

☐ If I have to be bribed to read, reading must not be inherently valuable.

☐ I'll hurry and just skim these books so I can earn some pizza.

☐ I can earn rewards if I act reluctant to do things on my own.

☐ These adults must not think I have any worthwhile goals of my own as a reader. Maybe my own goals are not important here at school.

The problems with extrinsic rewards are directly tied to issues surrounding grades and assessment (Thomas & Oldfather, 1997). For some students, grades may function in the same ways as the pizza in the food-for-reading program described above. Grades, rather than intrinsic motivations, can become the end, the purpose, the reason for taking part in school. As Akpene, one of Jane's students wrote, "I have never been a learner, because I have been so busy being a student." Akpene explained that her concerns about making good grades to satisfy parents and teachers superseded her own desire to learn or to make sense of the world.

Students construct ideas about the implications of grading that can surprise us. For example, in conducting a longitudinal study in Dorothy Rice's classroom in the rural southeast (West, 1996a), Jane was observing third graders as they worked on a word puzzle as part of their study of folklore. One child asked Dorothy, "Are you gonna put a grade on this?" Curious, Jane asked the child, "Why'd you ask that?" "I want to know if we can help each other," he replied. Not only do grading practices influence children's relationships with classmates (cooperative/collaborative or competitive; solitary or interactive), but grades also influence children's attitudes toward literacy enterprises. For example, the expectation of grades influenced Dorothy's students' experience of the activities as fun or as work, whether or not they had access to help, and their thinking about what mattered most in school.

Implications of social constructivism and motivation research ask that educators consider what kinds of practices will help students become involved in setting their goals, assessing their work, evaluating their growth, and thus gaining ownership of their learning. Students who have opportunities to participate in these ways may be able to focus on meaning and intrinsic purposes rather than on grades and other extrinsic reasons for learning (Kohn, 1993). Many educators are using alternative forms of assessment to supplement (or even replace) grades. For example, teachers may use portfolio assessment (Paris & Ayers, 1994), in which students take responsibility for selecting samples of their work that represent their learning. Students write reflections about why they chose these samples, describe what they have learned and why it is important, and what they feel they need to work on next.

Grades do not reflect learning across time. For example, a student may make a "B" each quarter in math for an entire year. What does that say about progress? The grade remains static. In no way does it reflect the dynamics of that student's learning, nor does it focus on the child's potential. John Dewey (1928) wrote poignantly about the importance of focusing on potential:

> Even if it be true that everything which exists can be measured—if only we knew how—that which does not exist cannot be measured. And it is no paradox to say that the teacher is deeply concerned with what does not exist. For a progres-

sive school is primarily concerned with growth, with capacities and experiences; what already exists by way of native endowment and past achievement is subordinate to what it may become. Possibilities are more important than what already exists. . . . The place of measurement of achievements as a theory of education is very different in a static educational system from what it is in one which is dynamic, or in which the ongoing process of growing is the important thing. (p. 6)

Unlike grades, portfolio assessment provides a means for students, their families, and their teachers to reflect on the student's potential, as well as upon specific information about the student's progress across time. Such alternative forms of assessment refocus attention away from grades (as an extrinsic goal) to a focus on the meaning, the specific skills learned, and the qualities of the student's learning. Some concerns about the amount of teachers' time required for portfolio assessment can be alleviated by giving the students some major responsibilities for these self-evaluative products.

THE PLACE OF ROTE LEARNING WITHIN A SOCIAL CONSTRUCTIVIST FRAMEWORK

The value of rote learning is not discounted within a constructivist framework when the learner can situate the learning within a meaningful context. We are all aware that rote learning is required to learn the multiplication tables! However, remember that understanding the *applications* of the tables makes that rote memorization meaningful and useful. Sometimes rote learning can become a means toward gaining conceptual understanding. For example, Penny remembers memorizing a list of prepositions in the eighth grade. Even after memorizing the list, she still didn't understand what a preposition was, and at that point, the rote learning served no purpose. Many years later, in the process of studying Latin grammar, Penny developed both a need for and an interest in understanding what prepositions were and what functions they served. Still able to recite the list, she applied the rote memorization as a means for deducing the function of a preposition.

SUMMARY

A teacher who holds a social constructivist stance focuses on learning as sense-making and not on the acquisition of rote knowledge that "exists" somewhere outside the learner. She is drawn to look at learning through students' eyes. When children's perspectives are at the heart of schooling, relationships between and among teachers and students are realigned (Lyons, 1990). Responsibilities for curricular decisions are shared, traditional hierarchies are

CHARACTERISTICS OF CLASSROOMS WHOSE TEACHERS TAKE A SOCIAL CONSTRUCTIVIST STANCE

1. A primary goal orientation of the classroom is collaborative meaning construction.

2. Teachers pay close attention to students' perspectives, logic, and feelings.

3. The teacher and students are learning and teaching.

4. Social interaction permeates the classroom.

5. Curriculum is negotiated among all participants.

6. The curriculum and the physical contents of the classroom reflect students' interests and are infused with their cultures.

7. Students' physical, emotional, and psychological needs are considered along with their intellectual needs.

8. Assessment is based on each individual's progression and not exclusively on competitive norms.

diminished, and the dynamics of classroom talk become more democratic. Students, as well as teachers, are respected as knowledgeable persons who bring important ideas to every learning experience within the classroom community. Realignment of relationships becomes possible when teachers' practices embody their respect for the integrity of each learner's mind.

RELATED READINGS

Belenky, M., Clinchy, B., Goldberger, N., & Tarule, J. (1986). *Women's ways of knowing: The development of self, voice and mind.* New York: Basic Books.

Delpit, L. D., & Perry, T. (Eds.). (1998). *The real Ebonics debate: Power, language, and the education of African-American children.* Boston: Beacon Press.

Duckworth, E. (1987). *"The having of wonderful ideas" and other essays on teaching and learning.* New York: Teachers College Press.

Fosnot, K. (1989). *Enquiring teachers, enquiring learners: A constructivist approach for teaching.* New York: Teachers College Press.

Kohn, A. (1993). *Punished by rewards: The trouble with gold stars, incentive plans, A's, praise, and other bribes.* Boston: Houghton Mifflin.

Nicholls, J. G., & Thorkildsen, T. A. (1995). *Reasons for learning: Expanding the conversation on student-teacher collaboration.* New York: Teachers College Press.

Oldfather, P., & Dahl, K. (1994). Toward a social constructivist reconceptualization of intrinsic motivation for literacy learning. *JRB: A Journal of Literacy, 28(2), 139–158.*

Perry T., & Delpit, L. (Eds.). (1997). The real ebonics debate: Power, language and the education of African-American children. [Special issue], *Rethinking Schools: An Urban Educational Journal, 13(1).*

Goal 2

Accessing Students' Thinking and Deepening
Understandings of Social Constructivism

Understanding students' thinking—seeing learning through their eyes—can transform what happens in classrooms. In Goal 2, we offer ways that teachers can (a) gain access to students' thinking, and (b) deepen understandings of the power of a social constructivist stance in supporting students' learning and motivation. Toward these ends we guide readers through the implementation of two strategies: the Children's Thinking Project (CTP) and thematic discussions of children's and young adult literature. The Children's Thinking Project involves conducting and analyzing a taped conversation with a student. Teachers who participate in a CTP often find that the experience changes the way they think about teaching and learning. The literature discussions provide an opportunity for teachers to explore issues of social constructivism and for young people to explore issues of how they learn. We provide an annotated bibliography of trade books organized around six themes for discussion: students' experiences of school, community and classroom cultures, inquiry as a way of knowing, consideration of multiple perspectives, motivation and sense of agency, and theories of knowledge.

A QUICK GLIMPSE AT A CHILD'S THINKING: CHRISTOPHER'S UNDERSTANDING OF LATITUDE AND LONGITUDE

The vignette below is an example of the kind of conversation that might occur in a Children's Thinking Project. This exchange occurred spontaneously in Jane's college classroom. As you read it, you will begin to understand how a CTP conversation might unfold. You can also imagine how classroom teachers might employ CTP-like interactions on a day-to-day basis with the students in their own classrooms.

One Tuesday afternoon in Jane's introductory course "Understanding Learners" at Agnes Scott College, students were preparing to conduct taped conversations with children. Working with partners to practice their techniques, the students were spread out in the curriculum library, the hall, and Jane's office. Jane looked up and saw Christopher, the fourth-grade son of one of the students, peering in from the hallway. Jane thought, "This is perfect! Maybe Christopher and I could model a conversation for the class." Christopher consented, so Jane called the students together and introduced Christopher to the class, including his surprised mother.

Jane: Christopher, maybe you could tell us a little bit about what you have been interested in, in school lately.

Christopher: Well, in social studies, we have been learning about land forms and maps and latitude and longitude and the Dead Sea, and stuff like that.

Jane: Great! What have you been learning about latitude and longitude?

Christopher: They're lines on the globe. And the longitude lines go north and south, and the latitude lines go east and west with the equator. The longitude lines connect the North Pole and the South Pole. You use 'em to tell where things are on the globe.

Jane: So, who would use latitude and longitude to tell where things are?

Christopher: (Pauses . . . He looks at the ceiling and considers the question.) UPS drivers use it.

Jane: UPS drivers use it. . . . I wonder how they do that?

Christopher: They look on the map to see where they're going.

Jane: (Pauses to figure out what to say next.) Can you think of anyone else who uses this kind of information?

Christopher: (Pauses again.) Bus drivers do.

Jane posed a few more probing questions to try to get Christopher to articulate his theory about the uses of latitude and longitude, but was not sucessful. After further conversation about some of the other topics he had mentioned, the class applauded in appreciation, and Christopher picked up his current book to read.

1 What does this vignette illustrate about Christopher's thinking?

2 What does Christopher know about latitude and longitude?

3 What are his conceptual "gaps"?

4 Based on what he has said here, what might his teacher do to help him construct a more refined theory?

Let's focus first on what Christopher *did* understand. He drew on his existing knowledge of how drivers use maps to explain that latitude and longitude are useful in locating points on the globe. He knew the difference between the two terms and their relationship to the equator and the poles. He grasped that latitude and longitude had some use for navigation.

What seemed to be missing from Christopher's framework? Admittedly, we have little to go on in analyzing Christopher's thinking, but we can hypothesize based on what he did say. If Christopher were in our classroom, we would investigate these hypotheses through further interactions and by observing the work he does. The following are some of the hypotheses we have formed: Perhaps he had not thought about how latitude and longitude were different from the way we use road maps. He did not distinguish between the more global functions of latitude and longitude and the much narrower content of a street map that drivers might use in finding their way around a city. The uses most of us might associate with latitude and longitude (e.g., navigation and rescue in air and water, hurricane tracking, or identification of specific geographic points on the globe) apparently were not part of Christopher's knowledge base. In other words, Christopher does not seem to have grasped the abstractness of the concepts he is describing. He may or may not be conceptually prepared to grasp these ideas.

In attempting to analyze Christopher's underlying conceptual structures, we bumped into our own gaps in understanding the functions of latitude and longitude. For example, we wondered how, exactly, are they used in navigation? Do ships' navigators still steer by the stars? Are compasses related to latitude and longitude? What computer technology is employed in navigation? Aren't measures of latitude and longitude in surveyors' schema? These questions reminded us that we clarify our own concepts as we seek to understand those of children.

This conversation with Christopher illustrates the myth that "teaching causes learning" (Weade, 1992, p. 91). Christopher had acquired correct terminology for the geographical concepts his class had been studying. He knew, on the surface, what those terms meant and could use them appropriately in conversation. He had the "right answers" and probably would have passed an objective test. However, when we look at the conceptual structures underlying his terminology, we see that he may not have understood in the way his teacher intended. Referring to this dilemma, Duckworth (1987) points out that Piaget's most important contribution to teacher education is

> in helping teachers understand that their students may be thinking of their subject matter differently from how they, the teachers, are; in helping them understand how their students are in fact thinking about it; and in helping them realize the importance of taking that thinking into account. (p. xiv)

Keeping this brief example of the conversation with Christopher in mind, we now turn to a step-by-step description of the purposes and procedures of the Children's Thinking Project.

THE CHILDREN'S THINKING PROJECT (CTP)

> Children's thinking . . . I am ashamed to admit that I never really gave this much thought. My job is to get the knowledge out there and they are to absorb it. I have to keep up with curriculum and assessment and make sure that everyone is "getting it." What do I care what they think? Am I ever wrong in this thought process!. . . This is what this project has shown me: A different side of me that I don't like anymore, and am going to change. Please read on and enjoy the complete metamorphosis that occurs.
>
> Kathleen Mazurek, first-grade teacher

The words above were written by Kathleen Mazurek, in her introduction to her report on the CTP that she conducted. The Children's Thinking Project (Oldfather, Bonds, & Bray, 1994) was conceptualized to provide experiential knowledge about social constructivism that is often missing in traditional teacher education. Many of us have been introduced to theories of Vygotsky, Piaget, and others, in ways that seem to violate the implications of the theories themselves. For example, memorizing and "regurgitating" Piaget's stages of development may not provide opportunities to construct understandings of the relevance of Piaget's work for your teaching and to learn to "think like Piaget." One of Piaget's quests was to uncover the logical nature of children's thinking and their cognitive structures. He gained valuable insight through simply observing particular children closely over periods of time and listening carefully to what they had to say. You can use similar means to gain information about children's current understandings of school curriculum as well as about other important elements of their experience such as their feelings, dreams, and relationships.

Conducting the CTP will also provide opportunities to reflect on Vygotskian theory and consider the relationship of language and thought reflected in your dialogues with children. You will be able to examine your role in scaffolding students' understandings. Our students who conduct a CTP often observe ways in which a child sometimes serves as a "more knowledgeable other" (Vygotsky, 1978), and scaffolds the understandings of children or adults. This experience expands on common thinking regarding the roles of both children and adults as teachers and learners.

> ## PURPOSES OF THE CHILDREN'S THINKING PROJECT
>
> 1. To increase understanding of constructivism and developmentally appropriate practices.
>
> 2. To explore a child's underlying conceptual structures and to examine their logic.
>
> 3. To develop skills in "getting into a child's head."
>
> 4. To consider how this project might have applications for your own teaching.

Procedures of the Children's Thinking Project

There are many ways to approach the CTP. (See, e.g., "Stalking the Fuzzy Sunshine Seeds: Constructivist Processes for Teaching About Constructivism in Teacher Education," which Penny Oldfather wrote with two of her graduate students about their experience in the project; Oldfather, Bonds, & Bray, 1994.) You might want to incorporate observations of a classroom experience, which you can use as a springboard for the conversation with a child. Alternately, you may choose to conduct taped conversations with children that you know through your neighborhood, church, friends, or family members. The procedures for carrying out a CTP are designed to include a conversation within the school setting; however, they are adaptable to use with students outside the school.

The procedures that our students have used are outlined in the display box. We also suggest some ways for conducting successful conversations with children and for interpreting what the conversations might mean for your teaching.

> ### PROCEDURES FOR THE CHILDREN'S THINKING PROJECT
>
> 1. Obtain permission for entry into the school.
>
> 2. Select a child and obtain permission of child and parent.
>
> 3. Prepare for the school visit.
>
> 4. Observe the lesson.
>
> 5. Conduct a taped conversation.
>
> 6. Transcribe the conversation.
>
> 7. Analyze the transcript.
>
> 8. Write report of findings.
>
> 9. Share with colleagues.

1. Arranging Entry

Arrange entry into the classroom through permission of the principal and classroom teacher. The kind of classroom you select will depend on your particular interests and objectives. Your considerations might include grade levels, teacher attributes, subject area of interest, and school neighborhood. Contact the principal and determine the requirements for making these arrangements. Written consent of parents and administrators may be required. Even if it is not required, obtaining written consent is the most ethical way to proceed in order to respect parents' right to know when their children are involved in projects such as this. We make it a practice to obtain consent from the child as well. (See Appendix A for Sample Consent Formoo.)

2. Selecting the Child

Consult with the teacher in selecting the child with whom you will talk. Alternately, you might like to select two children so that you can do comparative analysis. Choose a child who the teacher recommends as being particularly verbal and outgoing. Although there is certainly much to be learned from children who are reserved, our students have found it more difficult to get such children to talk openly about their learning. Other characteristics of interest might include gender, race, socioeconomic status, and relative success in school. Because young children's thinking is quite different from that of adults, you might find it fruitful to choose a young child, particularly if you are interested in early childhood education.

3. Preparing for the School Visit

Test all of your equipment in advance and practice using it. Be sure to have fresh batteries. You may want to bring an A/C adapter, to allow options for either battery or outlet use. Some tape recorders require an external microphone (that tend to result in clearer recordings). Collect materials needed for note taking. Select a dark pen that will allow you to write very quickly with a light touch. Look for a notebook that provides space for coding and marginal notations. Other materials that you may want to take are suggested in Item 5.

4. Observing a Lesson

Make arrangements for a date and time to visit the classroom and to take the child out of the classroom for the taped conversation. If possible, talk with the teacher prior to observing to find out the purposes of the lesson. It may also be helpful to spend some time making informal observations of the class as a whole, noticing, for example, children's and teacher's roles, and the general climate of the classroom. The teacher can help you find an appropriate place to sit. In some classrooms it is possible to sit with the students and remain unobtrusive; in others, you may need to remain at the back of the room. During your formal observation of the selected lesson, pay particular attention to the student's responses: interaction with the teacher and peers, apparent level of interest, body language, comments, written work, and so forth. Take careful notes of everything you observe, capturing as much detail as possible regarding your selected child. If you have never taken observational notes before, you may want to practice in another setting, such as a school cafeteria, a shopping center, your university classroom, or a family gathering. With proper permission, you may want to make an audio- or videotape of the lesson for closer examination. The teacher will appreciate a note of thanks for her help.

5. Conducting the Conversation

After the lesson, conduct a taped conversation with the child. If possible, try to avoid conducting the conversation during recess or other times when the student would be resistant to participating. If you have selected two children, you will probably want to talk with them separately. Choose a quiet location outside the classroom, such as the media center or a spot on the school grounds. In order to test the tape recorder and to put the student at ease, you might begin by allowing her to talk into the microphone and playing her voice back for her. Asking her to state her name and the date is a good way to document the conversation. She might like to play with the tape recorder a bit.

(This may get the urge out of her system.) To help put her further at ease, explain to the student the purpose for the conversation, as well as for the tape recorder and the note taking. Some "get acquainted" talk may help get the conversation flowing. If you are going to take notes, try to do so unobtrusively. Do not try to write down every word, but make note of particularly interesting phrases, and record what you notice about the student's manner, expressions, and actions that would not be evident from listening to the tape recorder.

But what will you talk about? Sometimes the lesson does not lend itself to rich discussion, so it is wise not to count on that alone. Rather, prepare a few ideas for discussion topics that are not necessarily related to the anticipated lesson. For example, you might invite a conversation about a scientific phenomenon, such as clouds, rainbows, the seasons, plant growth, or electricity. You could engage the child in a discussion about her favorite book, her writing strategies, or the geographical area where she lives. You could explore her views on the purposes of schooling. You might find it very productive to ask what advice she has for beginning teachers.

You could stimulate a conversation by taking along an object, such as a book, a balloon, a photograph, or an invention of interest about which the student could put forth some theories. Another option is to ask the student to participate in a Piagetian task and pursue a conversation based on that experience.

If the observed lesson is one that lends itself to a fruitful conversation, you could begin a discussion by asking, "What do you think your teacher wanted you to learn?" or, for example, "Why is it important to learn about photosynthesis?" "Were there some new ideas in the lesson for you?" "Did anything seem weird or surprising?" "What did you wonder about?"

Probing questions are some of the most effective. "How" and "why" questions that are based on what the child has just said can enable her to reflect more deeply and elaborate. Sometimes the conversation can be kept flowing by rephrasing a question in a different way, or simply to repeat what the student has just said.

Regardless of the approach you choose, the manner in which you conduct the conversation will have an impact on the quality of the talk. We hope that you and the student will both experience this as a natural conversation between two people, rather than as a prepared interview with a "script" of questions. You can show your natural interest in the student's ideas by your body language and the tone of your voice. Be sure that the student does not experience your conversation as a test of what she knows. Your manner and tone can make this difference. For example, you can ask a student, "What is photosynthesis?" in a "testlike" manner that may inadvertently inhibit a response, or in an interested conversational manner that invites the student to put forth his own personal theory. You might say, "I wonder what . . ." indicating that you are taking the role of a learner. We refer to this stance as "taking off the teacher hat." Keep in mind that the purpose in this project is not to teach the child about subject matter, but to discover how the child is thinking. Your goal is not to identify whether the student knows particular vocabulary and can parrot back an adult's words. Rather, the purpose is to learn about the deeper levels of a child's concepts and, more broadly, about the child's perceptions of what it means to be a learner, of what it means to know something, and of how he makes sense of himself and the world around him.

Occasionally you may find that having a conversation with a particular child is quite difficult. In such situations, we suggest that you politely complete the interview, select another student, and try again. Even if the conversation doesn't go as you had hoped, the experience as a whole can still be quite successful. The analysis and reflection that you complete later make the difference in what you learn from doing the project.

GUIDELINES FOR A SUCCESSFUL CONVERSATION WITH A CHILD

Before the Conversation

- Prepare a few ideas for discussion topics.

- Choose a quiet location.

- Test the tape recorder.

During the Conversation

- Put the student at ease.

- If you take notes, do so unobtrusively.

- Ask probing, open-ended questions.

- Reflect back what the child has said.

- Keep an informal, conversational tone.

- Show interest through your body language.

- Avoid "testing" and "teaching" the student.

- Above all, be a learner!

An Alternative Approach: A Conversation "With No Purpose"

Heshusius (1995) proposed another approach to talking with children. Her university students have participated in taped conversations "to create a situation in which the students have to deliberately meet and get to know a young person whose teacher they could possibly be, while keeping their teacher identities from dictating the interaction" (p. 117). In their analysis of those conversations, Heshusius's students were asked to "reflect on their most personal reactions to the assignment: What did the conversation illuminate about themselves? What did they feel, think, look forward to, worry about, enjoy, not enjoy, before, during and after the conversation and why?" (p. 117).

As in the previous approach, it is important that the conversation not take the form of an interview. The students participating in the conversations "with no purpose" learned that when they were able to blur the boundary between "self" and "other," they were more fully attentive to the child. They discovered common ground in "shared childhoods." The essence of what Heshusius concluded about her research was that "to hear youngsters, we must get ourselves out of the way" (p. 122).

Conversing With a Child Outside the School Setting

If you have chosen to have a conversation with a child outside the school setting, you will, of course, need to adapt the procedures described above. In this case, consent forms may not be necessary, as you will be making arrangements directly with the child's parents. You will also have more options about choosing an appropriate setting. Natural environments, such as parks, can be particularly conducive to productive and comfortable conversations. Other possible settings might include visiting a library or zoo, swinging on the front porch, or sipping a milkshake in the child's favorite restaurant. If you have the conversation in the child's home, try to arrange for a quiet room where family members will not interrupt.

6. Transcribing the Conversation

You will probably find that the process of transcribing the exchange will be helpful to you as a first step in your close examination of the conversation with the child. The transcription will be easiest for you if you can do it very soon after your conversation with the student. You will need to allow plenty of time. If you are a good typist, the transcribing will probably take about four-to-five times as long as the conversation itself. In the transcription, you will need to note overlapping conversation, long pauses, and nonverbal communication, such as laughter, gestures, facial expressions, and body language. Interruptions or other external events also may be noted.

7. Analyzing the Transcript

You will be rereading the transcript several times as you analyze it. As you read, remember the questions that guided your conversation, and ask yourself, "What is this about?" and "What is going on here?" What did the child want to talk about? Were they the same topics that you wanted to discuss? Why or why not? An excellent idea for this analysis was suggested by one of Penny's students, Alicia Lindsey, who used a Venn diagram to compare and contrast the interest and focus of each participant in her conversation. (See Figure 1.) As Alicia analyzed the content of the transcript she discovered the commonalties and differences in her interests and the child's interests in their conversation about television.

As you continue your data analysis, you might consider what the child's words reveal about her logic about the world. Are there examples in the conversation in which the child is exhibiting rote learning without conceptual un-

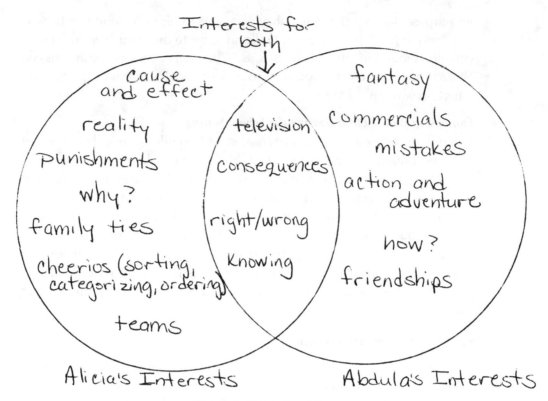

Interests for both ↓

Cause and effect
reality
punishments
why?
family ties
Cheerios (sorting, categorizing, ordering)
teams

television
consequences
right/wrong
knowing

fantasy
commercials
mistakes
action and adventure
how?
friendships

Alicia's Interests   Abdula's Interests

Figure 1 *Alicia's Venn Diagram*

derstanding? How did you uncover these? Analyze what role you played in the conversation: What did you do or say that helped or hindered the flow? Were you able to probe deeply into the child's thinking? The following is an excerpt from Jill's conversation with first grader Carmen about reading that you can use to consider these questions in relation to a concrete example.

Jill's Conversation With Carmen

Carmen is a first grader for whom Jill baby-sat frequently. Read the dialogue and consider the self-directed questions below.

Jill: Tell me what it's like to be able to read.

Carmen: Um . . . Well it's fun.

Jill: Why is it fun?

Carmen: Because you get to read different stories. And once you learn how to read, it's kind of fun. Just because, um, um, um, you could see the pictures, and you learn how to read the words.

Jill: Mmm hmm. And, um, do you get to use reading in other places, um, besides in your [basal]?

Carmen: Yeah.

Jill: Like where?

Child: On the carpet.

Jill: Mmm hmm.

Carmen: We learn to read on the carpet, actually.

SELF-DIRECTED QUESTIONS

1 What does Carmen's comment about reading on the carpet imply about her understanding of Jill's question?

2 How is this different from what Jill intended to ask?

3 How does the discrepancy between Carmen's and Jill's understanding illustrate key ideas of social constructivist theory?

4 What clues does Carmen provide about what she believes helps her read?

8. Coding Your Data

One way to sort out the ideas in your data is to use *coding,* a method of data analysis used by qualitative researchers: Recurring ideas are identified and labeled, or categorized. For example, in the transcript above, Jill noticed that the student was associating reading the stories with enjoyment. She named this category *feelings about literacy* and gave the category a code of FL. Jill also noticed that Carmen was aware of the functions of both pictures and print in contributing to meaning. She named the category *literacy awareness* and gave the category a code of LA. Each time she found an example of this category in her data, she labeled it in the margin with the same code. Jill also wrote marginal comments to capture her interpretations as she worked with the data. For example, in the Jill–Carmen dialogue Jill noted that Carmen was taking her question about places for reading quite literally in her reply, "We learn to read on the carpet, actually." Jill took from this that she needs to be more precise in her questioning.

> For more information on qualitative data analysis, see Related Readings at the end of Goal 2.

In your analysis, be careful that you do not jump to conclusions or make assumptions about students' intentions. Remember that you are learning about this child in particular, in this setting and on this day, and not necessarily about other children. Be careful not to generalize your assertion inappropriately. For example, in Jill's conversation with Carmen, it is reasonable for Jill to assert that Carmen appears to have a positive attitude toward reading. Let's examine Carmen's statement that "you get to read different stories." One might be tempted to interpret this as indicating that Carmen reads a wide variety of books. Based on her words, however, there is not enough to go on to reach this conclusion.

When you have completed your coding, try creating a concept map, or web, depicting the connections among the various categories. This can help you make sense of your coding by looking beyond the surface details to understand the "big picture" in more depth. Your map can serve as a wonderful basis for writing your report and sharing with others how you have interpreted your data. Your interpretations of the data will evolve as you spend more time with it. You may change your mind about your early interpretations. Debbie Davis, a second-grade teacher and Penny's student, had a conversation with one of her students in which they considered the potential effectiveness of a bug catcher he had designed. (See Figure 2.)

Debbie and Jonathan talked about his idea for an invention that catches bugs. Jonathan explained the purpose of his invention, detailed the types of

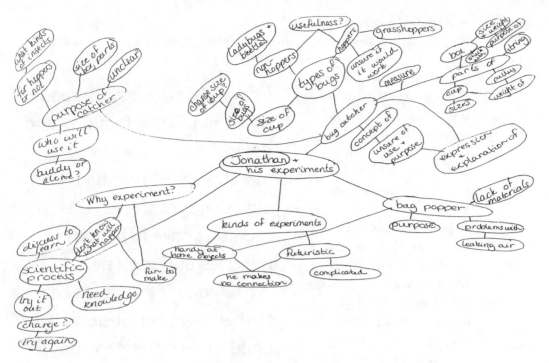

Figure 2 *Debbie's Concept Map*

bugs he could catch, and described the bug catcher's parts and how it would work. They also explored Jonathan's ideas about scientific learning through experimentation: why he likes to experiment, what kinds of experiments he has tried, and an experiment that had failed.

As you study your own concept map, you can step back and ask, "What does this tell me about the child as a learner? How might it make a difference to have this information as the child's teacher? What can I learn from this about the role(s) that I want to play as a teacher?" Debbie has included on her map puzzling aspects of Jonathan's thinking that are reflected in his uncertainty about some of their topics, such as why his bag popper is not working or why it is useful to know which bugs hop. The map indicates that Jonathan is developing a good sense of the scientific process and how he might apply it in his efforts as an inventor. For example, Jonathan asks questions, gathers data, tries out research strategies, and formulates classification systems and scientific theories about bugs. Stepping back from the concept map and considering her conversation with Jonathan, Debbie critiqued her own tendency to rush Jonathan during the conversation. In her efforts as a teacher to "cover" the material, she did not allow time for Jonathan to develop his thoughts fully.

9. Writing the Report

As your analysis evolves, begin writing your research report. You will probably want to start by describing the child, the context of the conversation, your methods of initiating the conversation and putting the child at ease, and the topic(s). Then describe your main findings about the child's thinking, your success in conducting the conversation, and, most important, your learning as a result of the project. The Guiding Questions that follow can lead you in writing about your findings. When our students conduct these projects, they provide us with the tape recording, a concept map, a transcript of the conversation, and the written report.

10. Sharing Your Findings With Colleagues

We often set aside time when students bring a rough draft of their report to class for peer review. We created a peer review form (see Appendix B) that students have found helpful in guiding their feedback to each other. Pairs of

> I have always wanted speed— speed in talking, thinking and doing. I have now realized that this speed may be causing a lot of confusion that shouldn't have to be part of the classroom experience. . . . We need to let children come to their own conclusions. . . . Children are going to construct their own meaning regardless of what we try to teach them at times. Why waste time giving them our meaning when they can just construct it themselves and probably remember it a whole lot better?
>
> Debbie Davis

students read each other's papers and then confer about suggestions for revisions. When revisions are made and the final papers are completed, our students share their findings with the class, read highlights from their transcribed conversations, and discuss what they gained as a result of participating in the project. We have found this to be a particularly important aspect of the project because students are able to benefit from the understanding gained by their classmates. The ideas of colleagues invariably spark new insights into their own work.

GUIDING QUESTIONS FOR WRITING UP THE CHILDREN'S THINKING PROJECT

1. What did the child understand about the phenomena or topics you explored?

2. What was the child's role in the conversation?

3. Did you probe beyond the surface and seek deeper levels of understanding?

4. What kinds of questions worked best for you?

5. How did you encourage the child to elaborate on ideas?

6. What might you do differently next time?

7. What additional questions could you have asked to enhance your understanding of the child's ideas?

8. What have you learned from this project that may help you become a better teacher?

9. What are the practical implications for your classroom?

10. What questions have emerged for you as a result of conducting this project?

Those educators who conduct the Children's Thinking Project often find that getting to know students in this way resurrects their own experiences as students. They gain a deeper level of respect for their students' ideas. Taking time to listen facilitates positive changes in their relationships with their students. Close examination of a transcript can reveal much that is missed in the press of classroom interactions, such as discovering the level of sophistication of children's understanding and the complex nature of their underlying conceptual structures.

Both preservice and veteran teachers who have conducted the CTP in our classes have experienced significant shifts in their views about teaching and learning. The following are excerpts from their written reports:

Slow down and enjoy that silence because that is where meaningful dialogue emerges. . . . I must stop thinking that silence means they don't understand.

Kathleen Mazurek

I think I experienced a role reversal. When I asked Michael about his favorite part of his birthday party, he told me, "Jumping in the Moonwalk." I honestly had no idea what the Moonwalk was. . . . Michael was not able to scaffold me. I guess I felt much like the new learner who is not getting the help they need despite the earnestness of the authority (Michael) to help me construct the new idea. . . . [Now] I realize that Michael actually did very well trying to explain it. He just didn't use one or two key words. How many times do I do that in my communication with children?

Letty Fitch

For me the most important part of this project is my realization of how much I love thinking about how kids think. I used to think teaching was making students understand the material—but through my own growth, this education class, and especially this project, I now know that teaching is about discovering how your students think and using that to help them construct their own knowledge.

Joy Garwood

Another interesting thing that I realized is how I misinterpreted J. because of cultural differences. When he was telling me about fixing the egg, I assumed he meant repairing it because that was what we had been discussing. He was using the term, fix, to mean cook, which is very Southern. Although we got our thinking back in sync, I know that there is an important lesson to be learned here.

Cyndy Piha

I used to have a perception that I knew a lot about Derek. . . . Yet doing this interview taught me that I really knew nothing about him. In fact this interview has only scratched the surface of who he is, and who he is helps shape what type of learner he is. I have learned so much about Derek, and about myself as a teacher and as a learner through this project.

Amanda Lockhart

SUMMARY OF CHILDREN'S THINKING PROJECT

Amanda Lockhart, one of Jane's students, wrote of her CTP, "I almost wish it was not as time consuming as it was, because I would like to do something like this for all of my students each year. What would be a better way to help shape your teaching each year to what your students know, think, perceive, and how they learn best?" She's right. Teachers cannot explore each student's thinking in this much depth. They can, however, become attuned to their students' minds. They can make talk about teaching and learning a regular part of classroom discourse. In their conferences with individual students, they can ask, "How's it going?" and "Tell me what you're thinking about this." Periodically, they can ask students to write journal entries about their thinking. They can become astute "kidwatchers" (Y. M. Goodman, 1989, p. 8). Teachers who are interested in their students' thinking use these and other ways they invent themselves to "get inside their students' heads" at every opportunity. Understanding and valuing students' thinking is not merely a matter of technique, rather, it is a matter of stance—of consciously choosing to see learning through children's eyes.

LITERATURE DISCUSSIONS WITH COLLEAGUES AND WITH CHILDREN

In addition to the Children's Thinking Project, another means for educators to inquire about social constructivism is through literature discussions. Toward this end we offer (a) a rationale for teachers' groups discussing children's and young adult books, (b) various strategies and structures for conducting the discussions, and (c) lists of suggested books and questions for discussion starters organized around the following themes:

- Students' experiences of school

- Community and classroom cultures

- Inquiry as a way of knowing

- Consideration of multiple perspectives

- Motivation and sense of agency

- Theories of knowledge

We also suggest ways for teachers and children to share in literature discussions that enable *teachers* to see learning through children's eyes and that help *children* become aware of their own best ways to learn.

Why Literature Discussions?

Literature can evoke rich feelings, images, and empathy, and become a vehicle for understanding ourselves and our place in the world, as well as the variety of perspectives and experiences of others. Literature can help us "to crawl inside the skins of persons very different from ourselves" (Huck, 1990, p. 3). Literature serves as a vicarious experiential basis for understanding different ways of being and knowing. Through carefully chosen literature, educators can explore issues of teaching, learning, and motivation. We can examine ways that roles, relationships, and rules are negotiated within the culture of classrooms and community. We can probe our own ideas, beliefs, and assumptions about what counts as knowledge and whose knowledge counts (Green & Dixon, 1996).

Why use children's books for adult literature discussion? There are many advantages. Children's books are easily accessible and are generally short. Beyond these practical considerations, many children's and young adult books address issues of importance to children and adolescents, and often present the world from their viewpoints. Young people are often the main characters.

We believe that discussing books is particularly appropriate to our purposes here in light of the social constructivist view of the relationship between thought and language. Literature discussion can promote *metacognitive awareness*—thinking about thinking—in ways that can make some of the theoretical aspects of social constructivism more easily accessible. These outcomes are not "guaranteed," of course, and much depends on the ways in which the discussions are approached.

Ways of Approaching Literature Discussions

Literature discussion can take many forms. Here we offer a few suggestions you may find useful in facilitating discussion of the themes offered in the following section. We love Karen Smith's (1990) idea of "entertaining a text":

> I talk to [students] at the beginning of each school year about "entertaining a text" the same way that they entertain guests in their homes. We reflect on the dynamics of this process and talk about how we often share advice, sympathy and laughter with our guests. We also talk about how important it is to listen to our guests and to try to think the way they do. (p. 20)

Approaching a text in this way makes it more likely that we will be able to enter the world of the story and see through the characters' eyes.

We suggest that prior to the literature discussions, participants establish some basic agreement about how the discussions will take place. Lively discussions will not be leader-dominated, and will provide opportunities for all members to participate in a safe and respectful environment. Most of us have been in groups that were dominated by a few members and know that it is easier to establish ground rules at the outset than it is to try to fix the dynamics after patterns have become set and particular individuals are dominating. The Related Readings section at the end of this goal contains additional resources for book talk among both adults and children.

Teachers can have discussions about these same themes with their students. Book talk with students in classrooms can provide another window to understanding children's thinking and social constructivism. Like the CTP, participating in literature discussions with your students is a powerful means of facilitating their thinking about learning and motivation and your own. Literature discussions focusing on issues of social constructivism can take place as part of the ongoing literacy program in classrooms, but will require some additional preparation and effort to add this new focus to the book talk.

The following are some strategies and structures for conducting literature discussions. These can be adapted for use in adult discussion groups or in classrooms with students. We have provided brief descriptions of each, and we hope that you will consult the original references for those you find intriguing.

1. *Literature circles* (Daniels, 1994; Short & Pierce, 1990) are small groups of readers who come together to discuss a book they have read. Sometimes everyone has read the same book or part of a book; other times, as in the *jigsaw* co-operative learning strategy (Kagan, 1997), each person has read a different book related to a common issue or theme. Discussions can be based on questions generated by group members (Commeyras, 1995) or posed by the leader in advance. If members have read different books, the discussion can focus on identifying different perspectives of the organizing theme. In our experience, however, discussions can take on greater depth when everyone has read a common text. With a common text as a base, further readings discussed jigsaw style can extend participants' thinking.

2. *Literature response logs* (Popp, 1997) can help prepare readers for discussion. Sometimes log entries respond to a prompt such as, "What is school like for Jimmy in *The Man in the Ceiling* (Feiffer, 1993)? What personal experiences do you remember that are like his?" In other cases, readers simply write what they're thinking about the book: what was going through their minds as they read, what was notable, what questions were raised, and so forth. All

group members bring their response logs with them as a basis for the discussion. We find that when students in our classes have written about a text prior to discussion, their thoughts are more fully developed, and the discussion is greatly enriched.

3. *Discussion webs* (Alvermann, 1991) are a way of structuring consideration of multiple perspectives on particular issues through the graphic aid of a web. Pairs of participants begin by generating as many points as they can to support both sides of a particular question and listing them on the two sides of their paper. The question should be one on which group members can take clear but disputable positions. For example, "Does the culture of Jimmy's classroom (Feiffer, 1993) support his intrinsic motivation?" Then groups of four participants compile their reasons and try to reach consensus about the issue. Groups report to the class, being sure to include any dissenting positions. Finally, individuals write their answers to the question, including their own as well as others' ideas. These written positions are posted for all to consider.

4. *Reading aloud* to the entire group rather than dividing into small groups allows a central text to be studied closely by all members (Cullinan & Galda, 1997). This shared experience provides a touchstone for subsequent learning.

5. *Sketch-to-stretch* (Harste, Short, & Burke, 1995; Whitin, 1996) invites readers to interpret through drawing what the book means to them (artistic talent is not necessary). For example, after reading Jimmy's description of school (Feiffer, 1993), readers might draw their conception of Jimmy in a way that depicts how he feels about himself as a learner in school. For example, one such sketch depicted a tiny Jimmy looking up at very large teachers, classmates, and family members, demonstrating the inadequacy Jimmy often felt. After examining group members' sketches and discussing them, the group might consider ways that the sketches have helped them see in new ways. When students engage in sketch-to-stretch, teachers have another pathway for seeing learning through their eyes.

6. *Think–Pair–Share* invites individuals to jot notes in response to a question, such as "What qualities of Jimmy's (Feiffer, 1993) experiences with cartooning exemplify his intrinsic motivation? How might these qualities become part of classroom life?" Pairs of readers talk about their notes and then share with the rest of the group for discussion. The group considers implications of the shared ideas for teaching and learning.

This is only a sampling of the ways in which literature discussions might be approached. Of course, you will adapt them to suit your needs and interests and add your own ideas.

Themes for Book Discussion

Smith (1990) pointed out that "it is often through interactions with others that we are able to create meaning in and about our own lives" (p. 20). Using some of the discussion strategies suggested above (or others you know of) you can use books for children and young adults to explore themes of social constructivism with colleagues and students. In Appendix C we have included an annotated bibliography of high-quality children's and young adult literature that are especially well-suited for such discussions. You will find a wide range of books for readers at all grade levels. As you consider the themes we have suggested, you will probably generate new ones of your own, and you will undoubtedly have your own book titles to add to the annotated bibliography.

We recognize that these themes often overlap; they are intricately interwoven, and the separations are artificial. For purposes of discussion, however, it is sometimes helpful to focus on one or two themes and explore those in depth. Although we have tried to consider each of the themes separately, discussions will likely uncover the natural connections among them. We have also included a few titles that do not fit the categories of children's or young adult literature, but are well-suited to the purposes of these discussions.

The following are descriptions of the themes and their connections to social constructivism. Suggested questions for discussion are provided, but participants are encouraged to base discussion on their own questions. As you read and discuss, try to consider each theme from the perspectives of the young people in the books. Consideration of the issues common to several books can stimulate a fuller analysis.

Theme: Students' Experiences of School

The books in this category provide a glimpse into what school is like for young people. Imagining the characters' experiences can help us think about the perspectives of students in our own classrooms and how they see themselves as learners. Seeing "through their eyes" can also allow us to take a close critical look at how we contribute to our students' experiences.

Suggested questions for discussion:

□ What is school like for the child or teen-age characters?

□ Do you recall similar experiences in your life?

□ How do the characters view themselves as learners? Are they confident, timid, adventurous, willing to take risks, self-conscious, resistant?

- How do their school experiences influence their conceptions of self? How do students' attitudes and self-perceptions influence their learning and motivation?

- Do the characters appear to be engaged in meaningful learning?

- What role does the teacher play in shaping the students' experiences?

Theme: Community and Classroom Cultures

These books can be helpful in thinking about how community is created and maintained. Some of them depict classroom culture particularly. Others depict culture and community in the world beyond school and provide useful models that might expand our thinking about life in classrooms. We all recall times when we had powerful learning experiences that took place outside of school; the books in this section might provide clues for how to bring "outside" learning into classroom settings.

Suggested questions for discussion:

Books depicting schools and classrooms:

- How would you feel if you were a member of the classroom depicted in this book?

- What behavioral norms are constructed by the participants in this school or classroom? How are these norms developed and maintained?

- What does it mean to be a good student in this class?

- What kinds of relationships do members have with each other?

- What counts as knowledge? Whose knowledge counts?

- What is the role of students in shaping curriculum?

- What role does classroom culture play in the students' learning and their overall experiences of school?

Books depicting communities beyond the school:

- What is community?

- How do the characters in the community in this book relate to one another?

- How is a sense of community developed and maintained?

- What are the various roles that individuals play within the community?

- How does this compare with your experiences in communities of which you have been a member?

- How might this model of community be useful in thinking about classroom life?

Theme: Inquiry as a Way of Knowing

A consideration of how human beings pursue their questions in the world outside of school—with no one dictating their modes of learning—can reveal ways in which meaning is socially constructed. Out-of-school learning can also provide a model for making learning in school more appropriate and meaningful through incorporating students' personal interests. Students can bring their own inquiries into the school arena and participate as collaborators in designing curriculum.

Suggested questions for discussion:

- What are the characters in these books learning?

- What questions are they asking?

- How are they pursuing these questions?

- What motivates them to want to find out?

- How is this similar to or different from learning in classrooms? How might this kind of learning find its way into classrooms?

- If these characters were your students, how might you draw in their natural learning interests?

Theme: Consideration of Multiple Perspectives

A primary tenet of social constructivism is the acknowledgment of multiple perspectives on an issue or phenomenon. Learning to value diverse perspectives has implications for developing empathy and respect for others, as well as for being able to consider new ideas. Seeing and understanding others' perspectives enables us to situate our own ideas within a broader framework.

Social constructivist teachers understand that their individual students have different perspectives, and that those perspectives must be respected.

Suggested questions for discussion:

☐ What are the different perspectives represented in this story?

☐ Are there perspectives that are somehow surprising or different from your own?

☐ How might these characters have come to hold these perspectives?

☐ How do their perspectives shape their actions, their learning, their views of themselves, and their relationships to others?

☐ If the characters had a better understanding of each other's perspectives, how might the events in this story be different?

Theme: Motivation and Sense of Agency

We have seen ways that social constructivist theory is relevant to motivation. An important element of motivation is the sense that we can set goals and reach them, that we can initiate action, that we can make a difference in the world—that we can be agents. The books in this section can provide food for thought about why human beings want to know, learn, and understand and about what supports our natural need for a sense of agency (Deci & Ryan, 1987; White, 1959).

Suggested questions for discussion:

☐ What goals do these characters have?

☐ What issues are of greatest concern to them?

☐ What actions do they take in relation to those issues and goals?

☐ What motivates them to take action?

☐ What conditions exist that enable the characters to believe they have the power to make changes?

☐ What inhibits their motivation to act?

Theme: Theories of Knowledge

Social constructivism is a theory of knowledge about "the relationship of the knower to the known" (Guba & Lincoln, 1989, p. 83). The books suggested here can help readers consider what it means to know, who holds authority for knowing, and how we come to know.

Suggested questions for discussion:

☐ What important knowledge do these characters have?

☐ By what processes and on what authority have they constructed that knowledge?

☐ What are the challenges to their knowing? How do they overcome those challenges?

☐ How does the characters' knowledge fit or go against traditional notions of what constitutes knowledge?

The literature discussions with students in your classroom may be as helpful to the students as they can be to you. Through their participation, students can become more reflective learners and become more aware of what kinds of experiences support their learning and motivation (Thomas & Oldfather, 1995). The discussions also have the potential to change the nature of classroom culture. They may serve as a catalyst for negotiated curriculum and realigned relationships.

Here is an example of how literature discussion might take shape: Jane teaches an introductory education course called "Understanding Learners," in which she and the class members explore diverse perspectives of students in classrooms. In keeping with the course focus, Jane chose the theme, "Consideration of Multiple Perspectives" using the book, *Who Killed Mr. Chippendale?* (Glenn, 1996). This book is a novel written in poems from the points of view of various members of the high school community. She read from the book each day as a springboard for discussion that very often took the form of think-pair-share. For example, Jane read diametrically opposed perspectives about Mr. Chippendale, a high school English teacher. After the first reading she asked students to write what they thought it was like to be in Mr. Chippendale's classroom. After reading the second perspective, she asked students to do the same thing again, and then discussed how to reconcile the two opposing perspectives of the teacher. On another day, Jane used a discussion web (Alvermann, 1991). She asked the students, "Was Mr. Chippendale 'burned out' as a teacher?" Drawing on the perspectives of the high school students in Mr. C's classroom, students worked in teams to prepare *pro* or *con* arguments and presented their conclusions to the rest of the class.

SELF-DIRECTED QUESTION

1 Look back at your participation in both the CTP and the literature discussions. How have these informed your understanding of social constructivism and ways that teaching and learning change when educators see through children's eyes?

We hope that your literature discussions with colleagues and students "create meaning in and about [your] own lives" (Smith, 1990, p. 20) in relation to teaching and learning.

Summary of Literature Discussion Approach

As the conversation with Christopher at the beginning of Goal 2 illustrates, we cannot assume that children's use of the "right" answers reflects deep understanding. It is important that we find ways to access students' thinking and to take that thinking into account as we search for ways of supporting students' learning. In doing so, we are not only supporting students' learning, but also are enhancing our own. Remember how we realized what we did not understand about latitude and longitude as we reflected on the conversation with Christopher? As Y. M. Goodman and Goodman (1990) pointed out,

> the traditional idea that teaching can control learning or that each act of teaching results in a reciprocal act of learning in each learner is too simplistic. Teachers learn and learners teach, and as they transact each is changed. (p. 235)

The Children's Thinking Project and discussions of well-chosen children's and young adult literature are two ways of focusing on students' minds and enhancing our understanding of social constructivism as a theory of knowledge.

RELATED READINGS

On Understanding Children's Perspectives and Conducting Classroom Research

Allen, J., Delgado, L., & Cary, M. (Eds.). (1995). *Exploring blue highways: Literacy reform, school change, and the creation of learning communities.* New York: Teachers College Press.

Hubbard, R. S., & Power, B. M. (1993). *The art of classroom inquiry: A handbook for teacher-researchers*. Portsmouth, NH: Heinemann.

Matthews, G. B. (1984). *Dialogues with children*. Cambridge: Harvard University Press.

Oldfather, P., Bonds, S., & Bray, T. (1994). Stalking the "fuzzy sunshine seeds": Constructivist processes for teaching about constructivism in teacher education. *Teacher Education Quarterly, 21*(3), 5–14.

Patterson, L., Santa, C. M., Short, K. G., & Smith, K. (Eds.). (1993). *Teachers are researchers: Reflection and action*. Newark, DE: International Reading Association.

Weade, G. (1992). Locating learning in the times and spaces of teaching. In H. Marshall (Ed.), *Redefining student learning: Roots of educational change* (pp. 87–118). Norwood, NJ: Ablex.

Journals Devoted Exclusively to Teacher Research

Teacher Research: The Journal of Classroom Inquiry, published by University of Maine, Johnson Press, 49 Sheridan Avenue, Albany, NY 12210.

Teaching and Change, published by National Education Association, National Center for Innovation, 1201 16th Street, NW, Washington, DC 20036-3290.

On Literature Discussions

Alvermann, D. E. (1991). The Discussion Web: A graphic aid for learning across the curriculum. *The Reading Teacher, 45*(2), 92–99.

Flood, J., & Lapp, D. (1994). Teacher book clubs: Establishing literature discussion groups for teachers. *The Reading Teacher, 47*(7), 574–576.

Gambrell, L. B., & Almasi, J. F. (1996). *Lively discussions! Fostering engaged reading*. Newark, DE: International Reading Association.

Peterson, R., & Eeds, M. (1990). *Grand conversations: Literature groups in action*. New York: Scholastic.

Roser, N. L., & Martinez, M. G. (1995). *Book talk and beyond: Children and teachers respond to literature*. Newark, DE: International Reading Association.

Short, K. G., & Pierce, K. M. (1990). *Talking about books: Creating literate communities*. Portsmouth, NH: Heinemann.

Goal 3

Envisioning Classroom Practices That Flow
From a Social Constructivist Stance

Constructivism is not a method. It is a theory of how we come to know, how we make sense of the world. A person who takes a social constructivist stance believes that *whatever* methods of pedagogy are used, students will construct meaning. To be sure, some methods are more likely to promote meaningful learning than others. The fact remains that children are always learning something. They construct meaning uniquely based on their own existing understanding.

In your Children's Thinking Project (CTP), you probably found that a child was able to use "correct" words, but constructed an unconventional and unique underlying theory. For example, during the time Jennifer's class studied Australia, we observed that Chelsea was able to answer many of the questions Jennifer asked about the country's wildlife, culture, landscape, and food. When coauthor Jill had an individual conversation with Chelsea, Chelsea went on to explain that there were no stores in Australia and that Australians were stranded because the country was surrounded by water.

> Constructivism is not a method. It is a theory of how we come to know, how we make sense of the world.

Social constructivism provides no map to follow, no teacher's manual, no scope and sequence chart. Individual teachers gradually evolve their own approaches as they get to know their own students' interests and needs and discover what feels comfortable for them. Just as our students construct understanding in school, we all construct a sense of how we want to teach.

In Goal 3 we invite you to personalize social constructivism by exploring your own educational history and by writing your learning autobiography. Relating your educational experiences to principles of social constructivism will provide a basis for looking at classrooms with a fresh view. Next, we revisit Jennifer's classroom and offer glimpses into other social constructivist classrooms. Finally, we suggest some practices that are consistent with social constructivist theory.

EXPLORING PERSONAL CONNECTIONS WITH SOCIAL CONSTRUCTIVIST THEORY

Most of us, if we are lucky, have had at least a few school experiences in which we felt capable and personally connected to what we were learning. At times our school experiences might even have helped us discover our passions for learning. We can examine our own educational histories to understand more fully the contexts that best supported our learning and motivation. Some of the following activities might be useful in reflecting on your own meaningful educational experiences. Adapt these activities to suit your situation, whether you are reading this book on your own or in a class or other study group. Select some of the following tools to stimulate your memories and connections, and to prepare yourself for writing your learning autobiography.

❑ *Mind mapping.* Recall a specific positive learning event in your life. Create a map or web that reflects the qualities of the teacher or the more knowledgeable other and the environment that supported your learning and motivation. You can then create a map that synthesizes the ideas.

- *Think–pair–share*. Individuals jot notes in response to the question, "What are your most memorable learning experiences?" Pairs talk about their notes and then share with the rest of the group for discussion. The group considers implications of the shared ideas for teaching and learning.

- *Time line*. Create a time line that represents significant aspects of your educational history.

- *Artistic representations*. Using clay, collage, drawing, or other media, create an image that symbolizes important aspects of your experiences as a learner and describe the significance to colleagues. You might even experiment with music, poetry, or other means of expression.

- *Treasured objects*. Select a "treasure" that represents an experience that has been important for you as a learner. Describe its significance to your study group. Put your thoughts in writing, if you wish.

- *Metaphors*. Develop metaphors that represent your school experience. For example, "If your junior high school were a vehicle, what would it be?" Compare and contrast that metaphor with one representing a different school context. Other useful metaphors might include the school experience as a television show, food, appliance, animal, season, vocation, artistic medium, furniture, and so forth. Or, make up your own! See how the vehicle metaphor played out in the following conversation with seventh-grader Lily as she described her positive elementary school experience (Oldfather & McLaughlin, 1993).

| **LILY'S VEHICLE METAPHOR** | Penny: If Willow were a vehicle, what would it be? |

Lily: It would be an old car. Something that you look at and you don't think it looks that great. You might think, "I'd rather have a Porsche convertible." But you get inside, and it's shabby, but it's very comfortable, and it's welcoming, and it's warm. It's not just a smooth drive. It's bumpy, and there's lots of turns in the road you're driving. And the driver isn't just sitting there. The driver talks to you. . . .

Penny: Who drives the vehicle?

Lily: Everyone takes turns. It's not just the teacher who's driving. Because lots of times the particular child, or a group of children, are leading the discussions that we have. It switches around to everybody.

Penny: Who reads the map? Is there a navigator in this vehicle?

Lily: The teacher. That's why she's there. She's the person who's able to maintain us, to keep us within range. That's the only difference. . . .

Penny: Where does this vehicle go?

Lily: The vehicle goes everywhere. It goes to all the countries, and it goes over the oceans and to Alaska, to Russia. It goes as far as it can go, and it never runs out of gas.

Penny: What's the gas?

Lily: The gas is the curiosity of the children. If the children were ever to stop being curious about the world, or being curious about learning, then the car would die. (p. 16)

☐ *Learning autobiography.* We have found learning autobiographies to be a particularly fruitful means of constructing a vision of meaningful learning. (For examples of teachers' writings that apply an autobiographical lens to their teaching see Hankins, 1996, and Portalupi, 1995.) Use your map, jotted notes, or time line as the basis for writing a memoir of your school experiences. Consider your own cultural life history as an important aspect of this.

For those interested in learning autobiographies, we provide an abridged version of an autobiographical story. It was based on the "learning history" that was written by Mariposa Arillo, one of Jane's students at Agnes Scott College. Mariposa chose to hand-write the original version on lined notebook paper, to evoke a sense of the child narrator whose voice she assumed. Following her autobiography is Mariposa's self-evaluation of this autobiographical piece.

THE UGLIEST

Fourth grade: I am the ugliest girl I know. My hair is not straight enough, and it doesn't even have the dignity to be curly. My teeth are crooked from sucking my thumb and from a wet-bathing-suit-and-a-slide accident. My clothes are hand-me-downs, my skin is a kinda greenish color that other people call "tan" to be polite, and I don't say the right words, or say them in the right way. I'm smart enough to notice that I'm not smart enough; not so short, but not tall enough; and definitely, definitely too skinny. There are lots of other things that make me the ugliest, but I'll tell you about them as we go along.

It happened all of a sudden, this turning ugly thing, because we have pictures of me when I was younger, and I was actually kinda cute. Part of it is that was when I was a kid, everyone tried to make everything seem good—there's this marshmallow gooeyness that grown-ups pour over everything to make it seem blurry-sweet. Like once my parents took me to a bullfight in Mexico City, and when it came time for the matador to kill the bull, my daddy took me to buy bubble gum. The *good* thing was that I learned how to blow bubbles that day. The *bad* thing was that I was totally in the dark about what really happened at bullfights. Mostly, though, my parents tried to be honest with me, but most grown-ups just tell you the good side of the story. When you find the whole truth you can't even be mad, or sad, or excited, cause you should've known all along.

From what I've managed to figure, grown-ups think that your major personality trait is that you're a kid. You know how people say, "I like kids," or "I don't like kids," like we all act the same? They think you don't feel or think the way *they* feel and think. Most teachers are especially that way—they think that who you are has to do with your age, or what kind of grades you make. They must think that on the inside we're like worksheets, and everyone has the same blanks that need to be filled with the same words. Grown-ups think you have to keep it simple 'cause we're just kids. Wouldn't they be surprised to know that we have our own world—full of laughter and teasing and feeling bad.

Then there's Ms. Knowlton. She's my Challenge teacher, where I go for "smart kid" classes. She's a different kind of grown-up, and her name suits her—she's definitely a knower. When she sees me in the hall, she doesn't talk real loud and make me feel like I should look down and mumble hello. She just smiles like we're sharing a special secret that no one else could know. She knows when to push us and when to wait, she knows our fears and our faults, and she is the only grown-up person at the school who understands what's happening in *our* world.

She never makes a big deal out of it, but she always knows what's going with us. I'm not sure I can explain what I mean, or even why that's important, but it sure is different from what we have in our regular classrooms. She knows that each one of us is special and shows us how we need each other for different things.

Like one time, when my best friend's parents were in the middle of a "difficult" divorce, Ms. Knowlton sent me and her to the library all day to make a picture book to read to the younger kids. How did she know that Susie didn't want to talk to anyone that day, and that in the library there were no teasing classmates? And the little kids loved it when we came in to read to them. How did she know that one time when Lionel wrote in the bathroom that he had a pair of Yoon's underwear? She made him write a report on slander, which is when you can get in trouble with the law for telling "untruths" about other people. But she didn't embarrass either one of them, because she never brought it up in class—I found out 'cause I saw him at the library "doing research." Anyway, that's the kind of stuff she knows—the kind that had to do with the world our other teachers couldn't see.

Around the middle of the school year, I began having a terrible problem that I couldn't explain to anyone. It was almost as bad as peeing in your bed or picking your nose or coming to school when your dad fixed your hair. Only this embarrassing thing no one could notice on the outside, not until I opened my mouth. That's when you could tell that my brain was caving in.

It all started one day in class when we were in our reading group. I was paired up with this really cute guy (who was so much older that he should have been in middle school or high school by now) 'cause me being good at reading was supposed to rub off on him or something. Anyway, out of nowhere, my teacher asked me to come to the board to write out a hard word from our reader. Then, just to torture me, she said never mind, I could do it from my seat. Well English is a difficult language to speak, but it is even more difficult to spell—and definitely harder to spell OUT LOUD. My mouth opened, but nothing came out. The only activity in my brain was that it kept opening up and closing in on itself, kind of like a hungry black hole. The silence kept getting longer, and the black hole kept getting bigger, 'til finally I blurted out, "¡No se!"

First of all I was embarrassed that I had to say "I don't know" in front of the whole class, but to make matters worse, I didn't even do it in the right language! Unfortunately, that was just the beginning. Every day, just when I needed it most, my brain would cave in and then there was nothing. I think I got this from my dad's sister, my *Tia* Edith, because whenever she really didn't want to have one, or was feeling nervous about it, she would have an epileptic seizure. This made her feel even worse about what she had been worried about in the first place. Now I could relate. Maybe I was having some kind of brain seizure.

The very worst part about it was that no one else seemed to notice, or maybe they just didn't care. But this is where Ms. Knowlton's knowing really came in handy. One day, just as class was over, she asked me to stay and help her put some new books on her shelves. She thought she was real slick, but I knew what she had in mind and my palms started to sweat. I knew that my brain caving in thing was making me not smart enough for her class. That's what she had to tell me. My *Abuelita*, my Mexican grandmother, was fond of saying that everyone had their cross to bear (only in Spanish) and I was realizing that mine was to be ugly and stupid—a not-belonger.

Ms. Knowlton smiled her knowing smile, and I felt the kindergarten kid (the one that cried over everything) in me getting unglued from the fifth-grade kid. You know how sometimes you have to squeeze your insides down to keep a secret or keep from crying? Well, I was squeezing and squeezing. I had to stop because she asked me a question, something I was not prepared for.

"Do you think you could do me a favor?"

Was this a trick question? "Yes . . . ma'am." (I added the ma'am part as a last attempt to stay in her class.)

"I need you to come in early tomorrow to help me."

"Me?" I asked, wondering how she could have confused the kid with the falling-in brain with all the really smart kids.

She did not bother to answer that, but confirmed by saying, "See you at nine!"

I was there at five 'til nine the next day wearing clothes that I could clean in, 'cause that's what I did when my mom asked me for help, so I figured Ms. Knowlton needed cleaning help, too. But she had a class full of first-grade heads bobbing up and down over puzzles and blocks. All of my hope fell to the bottom of my stomach, and I figured she had given up on me. She would not need my help after all. One of the heads bobbing up and down was covered by a graying afro—and I knew that was Ms. Knowlton. I wondered if I should try to slip out before she saw me. She must have heard me thinking, 'cause she looked up and caught me with her eyes. Her head (and her hair) waved me in her direction. She patted the seat next to her. Sometimes you don't have to talk to say what you mean, so I didn't talk, too. I just sat down next to her.

What happened next I won't try to explain, I'll just tell you like it happened. She touched my hand, and I felt the knowingness inside of her talk to the knowingness inside of me. I laughed. I felt tickled by my inside knowing, and I wanted to share this feeling. A teacher was born that morning. Me.

Mariposa Arillo
Autobiography
Edu 210
Agnes Scott College
10-7-97

The following is Mariposa's self-evaluation:

SELF-EVALUATION OF LEARNING AUTOBIOGRAPHY

After reading through your entire paper, evaluate it along these lines:

1. How would you assess the quality of ideas represented in your paper? How well does it portray something significant about you as a learner?

I think my paper represented my need to be recognized as a thoughtful individual—and that never happened in school. I tried to give an in-depth view of one time in my life, but it's kind of hard to be concise at the same time. If I could add about 5 more pages and maybe tie in some interrelations with my classmates—that would help.

2. How would you assess the quality of your writing? Think about style as well as organization and mechanics.

The most glaring problem is that I couldn't END. I really wanted it to contain the power and the magic of the moment, but I'm not sure I captured that. (I really wanted to use the note-

book paper to lend to the child's perspective.) I really tried very hard to stay true to some of the influences in my childhood.

As I read over it again I felt like there were 2 distinct parts—and in my life they both overlap but not necessarily on paper. My feeling ugly and my feeling dumb. (I really did not feel entirely comfortable with myself until I went away to college.) On paper it seems over-simplified and too like someone else—not me—even though its all true.

3. What have you learned in the process of writing the paper?

I really want to get in touch with Ms. Knowlton to thank her for being such a great teacher. I also remembered a lot of the pain and confusion I felt at that time. Really, it kind of helped me to come to terms with that experience.

> **Writing this paper has helped me put into words [some of my] thoughts and ideas that were only disconnected fragments . . . It shows me that writing out my experiences helps me learn from them and make connections I would not otherwise make.**
> **Olivia Roller**

Students who have written learning autobiographies are often surprised by what the process reveals to them. Some students, like Mariposa, choose to write about very difficult perionds; others focus on more positive memories. Virtually all report the writing of their autobiographies as a valuable learning experience.

> I think I need to mail a copy [of my learning autobiography] to Mrs. Pastorelli. . . . I don't know if I've ever flat-out thanked her. Maybe this paper would be a way of doing that. I've also developed more concrete ideas about how I can help my struggling students. I was, after all, a closet struggler.
>
> Jennifer Woodruff

> The experience [described in my autobiography] still haunts me today. . . . Putting it down on paper was good because I could read [it] again—kind of objectively look at [my former teacher] and say she was an awful teacher. I think there is a lot to be learned from personal writing. I used to think it was too

hard for me to do, but I am on my way to changing my mind. I thank you for the opportunity to do this assignment. I learned a lot about myself as a learner.

Amanda Lockhart

SELF-DIRECTED QUESTIONS

Those who decide to write a learning autobiography might consider these questions:

1 What are the main "themes" that emerge from your exploration of your learning history?

2 In what ways do these themes converge with key ideas of social constructivism?

3 How does your learning history influence the kind of teacher you want to be?

In Mariposa's case, her struggle with her self-image and feelings of inadequacy often come up as she thinks about the students in her future classroom. For example, in the class she was taking with Jane, she read a case study of a young writer. Mariposa's written response to the case study focused on what Mariposa viewed as the child's low self-esteem and its effects, such as the child's lack of success in school. In a research project she designed, Mariposa posed the question, "How do children construct self-image?" And in the analysis of her CTP, she wrote a great deal about the self-esteem of the child with whom she spoke. Mariposa's awareness of her own childhood struggles with self-esteem is becoming a lens for understanding children and will enable her to consider her teaching and her classroom from the perspective of her students.

Other people who have reflected about their learning histories often find that their best teachers were passionate about teaching, concerned about students as individuals, knowledgeable and enthusiastic, interested in what students had to say, and had a sense of humor. Other elements of memorable experiences often include those that involve real-world, challenging, hands-on experiences, or opportunities for physical movement, and those that make connections with the broader community beyond the school. Chances are that many of these experippences grew out of opportunities to make choices and to participate actively, as did Jennifer's kindergarten children. As seen in Mariposa's story, sometimes memorable learning experiences are not pleasant, but can be instructive to us as educators in thinking about the kind of teachers we wish to be and the kinds of classrooms we want to create. Examining your own learning history in this way provides an experiential base for constructing a vision of the kind of classroom you want to create.

"SNAPSHOTS" FROM CLASSROOMS

As we have acknowledged, a person who holds a social constructivist stance believes that learners are constantly constructing meaning, no matter what pedagogical methods are being used. Nevertheless, not all practices are equally effective in promoting meaningful learning. Even though social constructivism is not a method, teachers who take such a stance make instructional decisions that they believe will best support students' meaning-making. Picture the 6 classroom "snapshots" that follow. Which of these appear to represent a social constructivist stance on the part of the teacher?

1. A fourth-grade teacher holds a writing conference with one of her students.

2. Third graders are using flash cards to memorize multiplication tables.

3. Kindergarten children color photocopied outlines of the Australian flag.

4. A middle school teacher introduces a thematic unit on survival that will integrate math, social studies, science, and language arts.

5. A third-grade boy sits alone at a table reading a book.

6. A teacher stands before her high school physical science class, giving a lecture on waves.

At first glance it may look as if snapshots 1 and 4 represent teaching from a social constructivist base and that 2, 3, 5, and 6 may not. Let's take a closer look.

Scene 1

In her fourth-grade classroom, Ms. Preston is sitting alongside Marty's desk discussing his story about a stray dog that he had been trying to care for. She reads his story, using her blue pencil to call Marty's misspellings to his attention. Then she asks him a series of questions designed to prompt Marty to add more detail to his story. "What color was the dog? What kind of dog was it? How much do you think he weighed? Was his hair long or short?" Marty answers each question, and Ms. Preston suggests, "Good. Now put that in your story." Marty hesitates, and Ms. Preston reminds him, "Good writers use lots of adjectives." She leaves Marty to finish his writing. "She didn't ask me why I cared about the dog," thinks Marty, as he begins adding adjectives to his story and looking up the correct spellings.

SELF-DIRECTED QUESTION

1. If you were Marty, how would you feel about the writing conference? How might it have been handled in a way that acknowledged Marty's feelings for the dog and supported his growth as a writer?

Scene 2

Mr. Fenner's third graders have been developing mathematical concepts through working with manipulatives at their desks, planning the amount of food they will need to serve at their class Halloween party, and estimating the cost per person for party food and supplies. Yolanda, like several of her classmates, understands the concepts but is having trouble with computation. Mr. Fenner offers his flash cards to the students, who work in pairs, coaching each other on multiplication facts.

SELF-DIRECTED QUESTION

1. What conditions in this classroom supported the children's social construction of meaning even while engaged in rote memorization?

Scene 3

Jennifer's kindergarten students have been engaged in a month-long study of Australia as part of their school's spring "Olympics." They have investigated the land and culture of Australia by enjoying both fiction and nonfiction read-alouds, by using their own writing to explore concepts about Australia, by examining the large collection of books Jennifer has assembled, by composing an alphabet rhyme about Australian cultural symbols, and by telling and retelling "stories" of Australia, its people and land. A group of children are gathered around a table coloring photocopied outlines of the Australian flag according to a model that Miss Allen, the paraprofessional aide, has supplied. Jake realizes he has gotten his red and white sections mixed up. He checks the model again and watches it closely to be sure he gets the rest correct. Another child asks, "Do you color this part red?" The following conversation ensues:

Jake: Miss Allen didn't do it that way.
Tyler: Miss Allen made it blue.

Connie: But it doesn't have to be perfect.
Katherine: Miss Allen isn't perfect either.
Connie: It's your flag, your choice.

SELF-DIRECTED QUESTION

1. What makes this seemingly limited coloring activity meaningful for the children?

Scene 4

Mrs. Aarons begins her 2-hour eighth-grade interdisciplinary class by describing the unit on survival, that she has planned. She writes the goals for the unit on the chalkboard and, hoping to pique the students' interest, tells them about some of the activities in which they will participate: reading *Julie of the Wolves* (George, 1972) and keeping logs from Julie's perspective, writing reports on edible plants in their region, estimating the amount of water needed to survive in the desert for a week, and planning a hypothetical rafting trip and overnight camp-out. She asks Jesse to hand out her syllabus with each day's math, science, social studies, and language arts activities and assignments for the 2-week unit.

SELF-DIRECTED QUESTION

1. How might Mrs. Aarons have approached thematic study in a way that would have allowed the students to have a voice in the curriculum (within the required parameters)? How might she and her students have created a more authentic inquiry?

Scene 5

In Dorothy Rice's third-grade classroom, children are scattered around the room, reading books of their own choosing. Many have chosen to read with friends. Clusters of two or three children have gathered on the carpeted floor, at tables, or in beanbag chairs, looking at a shared copy of a book or reading multiple copies of the same book. They take turns reading aloud or read silently side-by-side and stop frequently to talk about their reading, to discuss an unfamiliar word, or to react to an unexpected plot twist. Cody, however, is one of the children who prefers to read alone. He sits in his regular chair at his regular table poring over the pages of a book about the sun. He reads silently, concentrating heavily on his own book, and speaks with no one.

SELF-DIRECTED QUESTION

1. How is social constructivism at work in Cody's solitary reading?

Scene 6

Members of Ms. Beam's physical science class have been exploring sound waves, light waves, water waves, and seismic waves. In their study, the students have used objects such as slinkies, springs, tuning forks, water troughs, radios, and bones from elephant ears. As the students are experimenting with the bones, Shameika asks, "What does this have to do with ocean waves?" In response, Ms. Beam gives a 10-minute talk, tying together the key concepts represented among the various forms of waves.

SELF-DIRECTED QUESTION

1. How does Ms. Beam's lecture differ from traditional notions of lectures?

Calkins (1994) calls brief lectures such as that of Ms. Beam "mini-lessons." She distinguishes them from traditional lectures in this way:

> Although mini-lessons often look like miniature speeches, like brief lectures, they are entirely different from the lectures that were such a part of my schooling. The difference can be summed up in a single word: *context*. In mini-lessons we teach *into* our students' intentions. Our students are first deeply engaged in their self-sponsored work and then we bring them together to learn what they need to know in order to do that work. This way, they stand a chance of being active meaning-makers even during this bit of formal instruction. (pp. 193–194)

Many of the activities that occur in social constructivist classrooms may appear on the surface to be very much like those in traditional classrooms. However, as in Calkins' comparison of a mini-lesson and a lecture, there are important underlying differences. These have to do with the *context* in which the learning enterprise takes place, and the *purposes* for which learners participate. The social constructivist teacher "reaches into" the minds of learners to tap their existing knowledge and build a basis for them to bridge to the next understanding.

> The social constructivist teacher "reaches into" the minds of the learners in order to build a basis for them to bridge to the next understanding.

Taking a social constructivist stance does not mean that the classroom culture is laissez-faire or that direct teaching is not occurring. As the classroom scenes presented earlier in this goal demonstrate, teachers with this stance are cognizant of their students' evolving understanding of concepts, are purposeful about their teaching, and are not afraid to take the lead when students need them to do so.

OBSERVING CLASSROOMS WITH A SOCIAL CONSTRUCTIVIST EYE

Now think about the experiences students in your class might be having. We are reminded of a story told by first-grade teacher Betty Shockley (personal communication, 1995), who had been searching for a way to help a struggling learner in her class. Finally, one day after school when all the children had gone home, Betty sat down in the child's desk. She took a look around the room, thought about the day's events, and asked herself, "How does it feel to be this child?" For Betty, putting herself physically in the child's place enabled her to take the child's perspective.

The questions below can be used to think about your classroom from the students' point of view and to consider what they might experience there.

QUESTIONS FOR ASSESSING A CLASSROOM FROM STUDENTS' PERSPECTIVES

☐ How does the classroom look? Is it a student's world or a teacher's, or a merging of the two? Is it a place I want to be?

☐ How do things in the classroom sound? How do I understand what the teacher says and does, and what my classmates say and do?

☐ What does it feel like to be a member of this class? Is it safe or scary, friendly or lonely, comfortable or rigid? Can I be myself?

☐ What are the rules? Who makes them? What does it mean to break them?

☐ What does it mean to be a good student? Is it following the rules? Knowing the right answers? Thinking carefully for myself and with my friends? Can anyone be a good student?

☐ Can girls and boys do the same things? How are we alike and different? How does the teacher treat boys and girls?

☐ What am I learning about ways in which people are alike and different? How are differences among students in my classroom treated?

☐ When do I feel puzzled? Engaged? Bored? What helps me feel interested?

☐ Are we engaged in important enterprises? Do we make connections with the world beyond the classroom? Does what we do make a difference?

☐ What are my purposes in learning? How important are grades?

☐ What counts as knowledge? Who decides?

☐ Can I make sense of things in this place with these people?

As you consider these questions in relation to your situation, the bottom line is this: Would *you* want to be a student in this classroom?

Characteristics of Classrooms Whose Teachers Take A Social Constructivist Stance

1. A primary goal orientation of the classroom is collaborative meaning construction. The focus is on sense-making rather than on a single right answer. Errors are viewed as a natural part of learning and as opportunities for growth. Teachers and students search for meaningful connections between what they know and what they are learning. Everyone shares the ownership of knowing. The teacher is not the sole authority for knowledge.

2. Teachers pay close attention to students' perspectives, logic, and feelings.

3. The teacher is learning and teaching. Students are teaching and learning. Everyone is asking questions and pursuing them.

4. Teaching and learning are based on social interaction. The talk is both structured and unstructured. The flow of ideas and information is multidirectional.

5. Within prescribed parameters of state and district requirements, curriculum is negotiated among all participants. Negotiation spans a continuum, sometimes with the teacher taking the lead, sometimes with the students taking the lead. They share decision making about important things.

6. The curriculum and the physical contents of the classroom reflect students' interests and are infused with their cultures. The classroom belongs to everyone. It is a place where people want to be.

7. Everyone is treated as a whole person. Students' physical, emotional, and psychological needs are considered along with their intellectual needs.

8. The teacher and students believe that everyone can succeed. Assessment is based on each individual's progression and not exclusively on competitive norms.

Summary

In Goal 3 we have invited you to consider your own experiences as a learner and to use them as a lens for examining your teaching. Perhaps you have been reminded of the ways in which your teaching honors students' voices, supports their intrinsic motivations, and facilitates their construction of meaning. And perhaps you have identified ways in which your classroom might be made more student-friendly, your teaching more attuned to your students' thinking.

RELATED READINGS

Atwell, N. (Ed.). (1990). *Coming to know: Writing to learn in the intermediate grades.* Portsmouth, NH: Heinemann.

Connelly, F. M., & Clandinin, D. J. (1988). *Teachers as curriculum planners: Narratives of experience.* New York: Teachers College Press.

Gitlin, A., Bringhurst, K., Burns, M., Cooley, V., Myers, B., Price, K., Russell, R., & Tiess, P. (1992). *Teachers' voices for school change: An introduction to educative research.* New York: Teachers College Press.

Grumet, M. R. (1988). Women and teaching: Homeless at home. In W. G. Pinar (Ed.), *Contemporary curriculum discourses* (pp. 531–539). Scottsdale, AZ: Gorsuch Scarisbrick Publishers.

Paley, V. G. (1990). *The boy who would be a helicopter: The uses of storytelling in the classroom.* Cambridge, MA: Harvard University Press.

Portalupi, J. (1995). Autobiographical understanding: Writing the past into the future. *Language Arts, 72,* 272–274.

Short, K. G., Schroeder, J., Laird, J., Kauffman, G., Ferguson, M. J., & Crawford, K. M. (1994). *Learning together through inquiry: From Columbus to integrated curriculum.* York, ME: Stenhouse Publishers.

Goal 4

Considering Possibilities and Challenges of
Seeing Learning Through Children's Eyes

Within this book we have presented ways to enhance learning and motivation when teachers make efforts to see learning through children's eyes. In doing so, we have presented some of the complexities involved. In Goal 4, our purpose is to explore in more depth the ways that such efforts can be both challenging and rewarding. As authors, we would do an injustice if we did not depict the inherent messiness of a social constructivist view of learning. We illustrate some of this messiness, as well as some solutions for making our way through it, by examples drawn from Jill's experiences as a beginning teacher struggling to hold on to her social constructivist beliefs in a school culture that does not tend to support them. Then we move on to illustrate ways that Jennifer has worked to effect school change through her role as an administrator in a school culture that is more supportive of her social constructivist beliefs. We describe a study of teachers' transformative experiences as they begin to look at learning through children's eyes. Finally, we report ways that teachers and students are applying a critical constructivist lens in order to bring about change in their classrooms and communities.

THE ROLE OF SCHOOL CULTURE: TWO CONTRASTING EXPERIENCES

We begin with the words of Jill Wilmarth, one of the authors of this book:

> I approached my first year of teaching equipped with ideas about democratic education and liberatory pedagogy. My interest in Religious Studies blended with my interest in education. Immersed in the liberatory works of Paulo Friere and peaceful activism of Gandhi, I was also knee-deep in the study of constructivism in my education courses. Theory began to feed practice for me, and I began to understand why my education professors and my Religious Studies professor taught their classes the way that they did. I came out of this experience, placing a high value on student voice. I gained a commitment to Gandhian philosophy that I had come to understand by taking Gandhian action. Members of our

Religious Studies course on Gandhi implemented his maxim, "Be the change you wish to see in the world" which was posted on a bulletin board on campus. For me this experience was powerful, liberating, meaningful education. Because I know what that feels like, what that means, how that works, I can attempt to bring this kind of education into my classroom.

Given Jill's philosophical stance, imagine the culture shock she experienced when she entered her first teaching position in an elementary school where her social constructivist views were not supported. Teachers at her school were expected to place heavy emphasis on teaching the tested skills—and little else. For each lesson that Jill taught, she was required to post on the chalkboard the objective to which it corresponded on the Iowa Test of Basic Skills. The students in the school had experienced a transmission model of learning.

When Jill invited her fourth-grade students to write about how they defined good teaching, the following response was not uncommon: "I think [good teaching is] when they do what who ever's in' charge tells them to do. And they teach wright [sic]." Jill discovered that these students had done little or no group or collaborative work and expected learning to be a strictly individual matter. They even erected physical barriers so that others could not see what they were doing. Jill observed that her students had learned a kind of helplessness and expected to be, in her words, "told where to sit and what to do."

Jill found that her students did not expect to participate in decision making: That was not part of the culture of their school. Instead, Jill was required to have rules posted on the wall and to participate in the school's reward-based discipline plan. She explained, "I don' t necessarily agree with it, but as a first year teacher, it makes it a lot easier for me to manage." As a social constructivist, Jill would rather work toward helping her students base their actions on a sense of responsibility to the learning and well-being of the classroom community rather than relying on a behaviorist management system. Near the end of her second year of teaching Jill planned to leave this school and searched for a school environment more compatible with her social constructivist stance. She coped with the difficult situation by making a few quiet changes in her classroom, such as instituting a writing workshop (Calkins, 1994). She also depended heavily on the support of her colleagues, many of whom shared her frustration. This group of teachers formed what Jill called "a strong, cooperative team" who used diverse approaches but who learned from each other and helped each other "make it through the day." These struggles represent some of the messiness encountered by teachers whose social constructivist stance is at odds with the culture of their school.

The difficulties may be even greater for teachers in high schools where there is generally a strong tradition of teaching-as-transmission (Oldfather & Thomas, 1998).

Contrast this with Jennifer's experience of a supportive school culture at Benton Elementary. Readers of this book have become acquainted with Jennifer's social constructivist philosophy through the descriptions of her kindergarten classroom. Let's consider her story. Her values and ways of knowing as a teacher and administrator can be traced from her early years as a student. The theme of learning as a social phenomenon surfaced in a personal narrative Jennifer wrote about her experiences as a student:

> My fondest memories of school came from the teachers' classrooms where the adults were having fun in their own classrooms. As a student, I enjoyed the teachers who smiled and laughed a lot, who had active learning projects, who allowed students to "open their mouths" from time to time.

Like Jill, Jennifer's undergraduate experience took place in a constructivist program; she was well-prepared to enter Benton during its shift away from transmission-style teaching. In fact, as a first-year teacher, she became an instructional leader because of her progressive educational preparation. Two years ago, when Jennifer was teaching kindergarten, she described what she was hoping to achieve in her teaching:

> I like to make a classroom a community, and to make it like a family, where there's a lot of social interaction. I don't plan on it being quiet. I want an active room. I feel the children can learn as much from each other as they can learn from the teacher, so I feel that it's important that they are always communicating with each other.

In her role as an administrator, Jennifer has continued her efforts to establish community and involve participants so that they can learn from each other.

> As Assistant Principal of Instruction, it is my role to provide staff development throughout the year that is connected to our schoolwide instructional goals and that provides focus on district-level mandates. However, it is also important to me that our faculty be able to work toward accomplishing these goals in a way that is not discouraging. So I want teachers (rather than me) to take the lead. Teachers have a wealth of information to share with each other.

We have a faculty committee that oversees instructional issues. In our first staff development meeting this year, the committee gave an overview of all our instructional goals for the year and our plans to meet those goals. Our way of doing this is to set up meetings in which teachers teach each other. I have a sign-up folder outside my office door labeled "Instructional Meetings," and teachers request topics that they want to learn more about or suggest topics that they may want to share with others. In the meetings so far this year, teachers have discussed reading and writing strategies that have worked for them, and ways of working in teams to meet learners' needs in writing workshop. The second-grade teachers confessed how they used to dread teaching writing workshop in their rooms, but now with the help of the support teacher it has become their favorite part of the day. A third-grade teacher, a fifth-grade teacher, and I, shared about ways that writing workshop connects to the State Writing Assessment for grades three and five. In an upcoming meeting, teachers who have attended conferences will share the strategies they learned there. Another session will focus on multiple intelligences, and will be conducted by two teachers who are being certified to teach gifted students.

It has been very exciting to sit back and discover the wealth of knowledge shared at these teacher-led instructional meetings. It has been a positive experience to have teachers volunteering to share information and strategies with each other in a nonthreatening environment, and to have our meetings based on the needs and interests of the faculty. Of course I had thought of things that I might share with teachers, but there hasn't been time yet. I don't mind this at all. It's more important to continue the professional dialogue that the teachers are sharing within the school.

There are direct parallels between the ways that Jennifer respected the ideas and interests of her students and the ways that she now functions in her role as an administrator. Within the parameters specified by her school district, she provides opportunities for teachers to take leadership of what they need to know and share to grow professionally.

In contrast to Jill, Jennifer entered an environment as a new teacher that was more in keeping with her educational goals and epistemological stance. Jennifer experienced support for her goals from administrators and colleagues. Because of the changing school culture, her students welcomed her innovations. Teachers wanting to move toward practices that flow from a constructivist stance need to keep in mind that things will be more difficult if they are teaching against the grain of the school culture.

SELF-DIRECTED QUESTIONS

1 Think about a school you know well. How would you describe the culture of this school? Is it more like that of Jill's school, where teachers are expected to transmit knowledge to their students, or does it resemble the culture of Jennifer's school in which students take more active roles in their learning?

---

2 Do a 5-minute freewrite about the school you have in mind. What are the implications of the school culture for actions you would want to take and for your feelings as a teacher within this school?

POTENTIAL FOR TRANSFORMATIVE EXPERIENCES FOR TEACHERS

As we have seen, social constructivist approaches do not lend themselves to convenient recipes or predictable outcomes. They require an emphasis on process, inquiry, negotiation, as well as a tolerance for ambiguity. Teachers who make a shift in that direction may find this difficult at first. However, doing so can enable teachers to enrich their professional lives in transformative ways. For example, Thomas (1994) collaborated with elementary teachers who were making efforts to shift the focus of their teaching to students' thinking. Part of their effort included use of the *California Learning Record* (CLR); (Barr & Syverson, 1994) and the *Primary Language Record* (PLR); (Barrs, Ellis, Hester, & Thomas, 1989) from which it was adapted. The teachers working with Thomas used either the PLR or CLR with two or three of their elementary students. The PLR was developed in England as a means of providing teachers, students, and their families with a holistic assessment instrument that was completely integrated with the teaching and learning process. The PLR instrument, in booklet form, guides the assessment, and thus the teaching, of literacy. The booklet includes questions about what children can do, emphasizing their strengths rather than deficits. The PLR involves documentation across time of students' progess by teachers, students, and parents. The PLR draws from the cultural funds of knowledge (Moll & Gonzalez, 1994) of the family. Early in the school year, the teacher meets with each child's parents and asks, "What's important for me to know about your child? What are your child's strengths? What does your child love? How can I help your child?" In this way, the PLR helps to establish a reciprocal relationship between school and home. Students conduct self-assessment and are involved in collaborative goal setting with the teacher.

The teacher collaborators in Thomas' study discovered that through their attention to children's thinking they made major shifts in their thinking about teaching and in their relationships with the children. Margaret, who had taught for 35 years, commented about some of the changes that she experienced in her teaching when she looked at learning through children's eyes. "I don't know if the word 'friends' [is what I want]. It is a different sort of relationship than I've ever had with the children. Comfortable. I just feel that they trust me" (Thomas, 1994, p. 168). Margaret continued:

> I began to see them as little ones who could direct their own learning. They are wanting to learn. I began to relax as I saw they wanted to learn. I see us not so much as teacher and children, but all more exploring together. And I didn't put so much burden on myself. . . . You can sum it up with [asking the question] "why" and trusting the children. Those are the two things that have moved the most. Yet if you'd told me when we started [this research] that this was going to help, I would have said, 'Oh, Sally, I already do!' So it's really interesting—the depth of it. All my life I've wanted this so much and danced with it, and now I'm never going to lose what I've gained. (p. 168)

The teachers saw strengths in children that they had not seen before their close observations. Teachers and students alike seemed to have raised their expectations. Margaret commented, "I found the more I ask them [questions], the better they do. What amazed me was that once I began writing down what they were saying and asking questions and just kind of keeping an eye on the different activities they chose, they began to get more serious about their work" (p. 168).

The teachers collaborating with Thomas found teaching to be more satisfying. They saw increased growth in learning in their students. They felt that their roles as teachers were transformed through making this shift. Thomas' research provides cases illustrating that when teachers attend closely to children's thinking and learning, it may not feel initially easy or comfortable, but this effort can result in enormously satisfying outcomes. We turn now to ways that social constructivist theory can support empowerment of teachers and students for taking democratic action.

DEMOCRATIC CLASSROOMS AND SOCIAL CONSTRUCTIVISM

One of the most compelling possibilities offered by social constructivism is that of education for democracy. In her article on that subject, Edelsky (1994) called for a kind of education that has as an explicit goal the attainment of a true democracy. This democratic education would support students in becoming capable of taking action for social change for their own or others' well-being (J. Goodman, 1989). According to Kuzmic (1993), the purposes of schooling are much broader than developing job skills and preparing for participating in our existing political system; rather, schools should prepare people for challenging the inequalities that exist in our society. Edelsky wrote, "Progressive language educators help kids become literate, but we don't necessarily make them critical" (1994, p. 255). We believe this charge is equally applicable across the

> We are not just socially constructing any meaning; we are socially constructing particular meanings in particular times and places, within particular sociopolitical contexts.

curriculum. The best interest of our students is served if we attend not only to the social construction of meaning, but also to the taking of a critical stance toward that meaning. We are not just socially constructing *any* meaning; we are socially constructing particular meanings in particular times and places, within particular sociopolitical contexts. When classrooms become places of democracy, when students can experience "meaningful participation in the decision-making that affects [their] lives" (Shannon, 1993, p. 90), our students can begin to take charge of their learning and their lives.

Social constructivist classrooms offer exciting possibilities for supporting democratic ideals through pedagogy as well as through curriculum. For example, in an integrated literacy and social studies course that Jane and her colleague Julie Weisberg are teaching collaboratively, student teachers are engaging in inquiry into biography with children in elementary and middle school classrooms. The course has highlighted issues of education for democracy, and the students' inquiries almost always have a democratic lens. Among the inquiries in this particular semester is that of Michelle and a class of fifth graders exploring biographies of peacemakers in their study of conflict resolution. Patrice and a group of fourth graders are investigating heroes: who the children's heroes are, how their choices have been influenced by the media, what makes someone worthy of being a hero. Julia has been reading biographies of Christopher Columbus with another group of children, considering both his heroic qualities and his flaws, and researching the effects of the Europeans' arrival on the Native Americans. In a fourth-grade Georgia history class, Neema and her students are researching personal narratives of women slaves in the pre-Civil War South. All these inquiries have grown from the social constructivist base of the college students. The students wrote proposals describing the inquiries they had in mind. They negotiated their plans with Jane and Julie and with the co-operating classroom teachers, and each inquiry has taken on a new shape as the children have become involved and made it their own. The children in those classrooms are socially constructing concepts and skills related to learning language arts and social studies, and they are doing so in ways that assist them in becoming more effective, critical citizens who are able to take social action on their own and others' behalf. For another example of education for democracy in teacher education see West, Willmarth, Crumley, Dickerson, and Francis (1999).

In each of the examples described, the social constructivist foundation is enhanced by the overlaying of themes of democracy and social justice in action. In another example of action research, a group of teachers we know has responded directly to Edelsky's call to create professional networks to support education for democracy. They have formed a study group called Literacy Educators for a Democratic Society (LEADS). They meet regularly to discuss books and articles they have read, pose questions, plan for action in their classrooms, and share problem solving and celebrations.

The group has generated a book (J. B. Allen, 1999) that will be of value to others who share such interests. The projects have involved group members' students in social critique. For example, in one class Mollie Trotman conducted an investigation with her gifted middle schoolers in which they examined the nature of giftedness and considered issues of their own privilege as members of this special class within a framework of social justice. In another, Barbara Michalove and her fourth-grade students studied racial prejudice on the playground, in the lives of their families, and in their classroom.

In a separate project, Holly Ward's (1996) fifth graders at Benton Elementary School took on researcher roles and examined questions that connect directly to their lives in school: They asked, for example, "How do kids learn to read?" "How can we get an after-school program?" "How can we change the athletic program?" (p. 65). Important changes, such as additions to the athletic program and plans for an after-school program, are occurring in the school as a result of the students' action research in this setting where adults listened to students' voices.

SELF-DIRECTED QUESTION

1. Considering the examples above, brainstorm some possible directions for democratic inquiry that might be appropriate for students with whom you work or might work in the future. What questions might your students raise for exploration that would involve them in social critique? In examining issues of social justice? In taking action to make change in their own environments?

A social constructivist perspective supports the goals of education for democracy. Both share a view of the learner as an active meaning maker. Both support the notion of learning as a social enterprise in which our ideas are connected to the ideas of others, both past and present. Both assume individuals' authority for knowing and decision making, and both value each person's voice and perspective. School settings in which students are expected merely to take in information stand little chance of educating for democracy. Instead, such settings educate students for compliant, automaton-like participation in society—citizens who feel they have no voice and no power for making change. Education for democracy requires schooling which encourages students to make important decisions, to understand multiple perspectives, to ask big questions and seek to construct answers, to believe that they can know things and act on their knowing (Nicholls, 1989). J. Goodman (1992) asserted that all participants in a democratic educational endeavor must have a voice in determining direction, access to knowledge, and access to communicative forums.

To summarize, social constructivism—with its implications of shared decision making, negotiated curriculum, teacher- and student-generated inquiry, and co-constructed knowledge—converges with goals of education for democracy. These goals support students' meaningful learning, their intrinsic motivations, and their constructive roles as agents of change.

Summary

There are both challenges and opportunities encountered when teachers take a social constructivist stance in their classrooms. Particular school cultures either support or thwart these efforts. When social constructivist teachers involve their students in education for democracy, their classrooms can be transformed. In the words of educational philosopher Maxine Greene,

> [An] important dimension of all education must be the intentional bringing into being of norm-governed situations, situations in which students discover what it is to experience a sense of obligation and responsibility, whether they derive that sense from their own experiences of caring and being cared for or from their intuitions and conceptions of justice and equity. (1995, p. 66)

RELATED READINGS

Allen, J. B. (Ed.). (1999). *Class actions: Teaching for social justice in elementary and middle school.* New York: Teachers College Press.

Edelsky, C. (1994). Education for democracy. *Language Arts, 71,* 252–256.

Goodman, J. (1992). *Elementary schooling for critical democracy.* Albany, NY: State University of New York Press.

Greene, M. (1995). *Releasing the imagination: Essays on education, the arts, and social change.* San Francisco: Jossey-Bass.

Shannon, P. (1993). Developing democratic voices. *The Reading Teacher, 47,* 86–94.

Ward, H. (1996). Kids on the move for research: Fifth graders' experience with action research. *Teacher Research: The Journal of Classroom Inquiry, 4*(1), 63–68.

final review

Social constructivism requires that we see learning through children's eyes. We believe that such a stance creates new possibilities for intrinsic motivation and meaningful learning. In this book we have defined social constructivism as a view of knowledge in which learning is constructed through social interaction. A social constructivist view focuses on learning as sense-making within particular sociocultural contexts, rather than acquisition of knowledge from some external source. We have also suggested various means for building understandings of social constructivism, including the Children's Thinking Project and thematic discussion of children's literature. We have provided examples from classrooms to illustrate the implications of social constructivist theory for teaching and learning. Finally, we have considered the challenges and possibilities of social constructivism through the eyes of Jennifer, a school administrator and former teacher, and Jill, a new teacher.

The following principles about the relationship between thought and language, derived from the work of Vygotsky (1978), form a basis for social constructivist theory.

☐ We acquire and use language socially.

☐ Language is the basis for thought.

☐ Therefore, sense-making (learning) has sociocultural roots.

Understanding the relationship between thought and language leads to the realization of the vital importance of culture(s) in learning. These include students' diverse home cultures as well as the shared classroom and school cultures. There are often gaps between the language and culture of home and the language and culture of the school, gaps that the teacher must recognize and bridge in order to help students connect who they are to what they do in school. Classroom culture, which is reflected in the way that talk takes place, has great importance for the ways that students view their roles as thinkers, knowers, and doers. Teachers are central to the establishment and maintenance of classroom culture, and students play a role as well. Traditional teacher–student relationships are realigned as teachers and students share ownership of knowing and students gain a sense of self-determination. Particular school cultures can have an impact on classroom cultures.

In a classroom where the teacher takes a social constructivist stance, collaborative meaning construction is a primary goal. The teacher pays close attention to students' thoughts and feelings. Both teacher and students are learning and teaching. Social interaction is at the core of teaching and learning. Relationships are important. Responsibility for listening and responding is shared by teacher and students. Curriculum is negotiated. Decision making is shared. The classroom and curriculum reflect students' interests and cultures. The classroom belongs to everyone and is a place where people want to be.

As this description illustrates, *social constructivism is not a method.* Rather, it is a view of learning that gives teachers a theoretical basis for making decisions about pedagogy and curriculum. We hope that we have made a successful case that theory matters, and that teachers' views of knowledge as constructed are critical in establishing classroom cultures in which meaningful, motivated learning takes place and democratic principles are embodied.

Appendix A

Sample Consent Form for
Children's Thinking Project

Dear Parents,

I am writing to request your permission for your child to participate in a children's thinking project with a student who is in my teacher preparation course at _____. My students will be going to _____ Elementary School to observe classrooms and to have conversations with some of the children.

Purpose: The purpose of the students' assignment is to learn how to access children's logic and appreciate the way they make sense of things. This activity is not for purposes of research, but is simply to provide a learning experience for the student. The children usually enjoy this opportunity to have individual attention from a college student.

Procedures: The student will observe the classroom and then will invite your child to have a 10–15 minute taped conversation in the school media center. The conversation will be transcribed, and the education student will use the transcription to analyze the success of interacting with the child. Your child's real name will not be used by the student in any written or oral communication about the project. A pseudonym will be selected, instead. When the assignment is completed, the tape will be destroyed.

continued on next page

If you are willing to let your child participate in this activity, please sign and return the form below within the next 2 days. For further information about the project, please feel free to contact me. I can be reached at_____ (office) or _____ (home). Thank you for considering this request.

Sincerely,

[Instructor]

If you are willing for your child to participate, please sign this form and return to your child's teacher at _____ School within the next two days.

I hereby give permission for my student, _____ to participate
                                          (first name)   (last name)

in the Children's Thinking Project with a teacher education student from Dr. _____'s course. I understand that the tape of the conversation will be destroyed when the project is completed, and that my child's real name will not be used.

_____   _____
(Parent or Guardian Signature)   (Date)

_____   _____
(Student Signature)   (Date)

Appendix B

Children's Thinking Project
Review Form

Reviewer _____

Who is the author of the paper you are reviewing? _____

Was there a complete draft of the paper? _____

Was the transcript completed and typed? _____

Check to Insure That the Required Elements (Listed Below) Are Included in the Paper:

_____ A description of the child, the context, and the topic(s) of the conversation.

_____ Processes for initiating the conversation and putting the children at ease.

_____ Assessment of the children's understanding of the topics or phenomena explored.

_____ An assessment of success in communicating with the children about their thinking.

Questions:

____ Were you able to get out of the teacher role, and let the child take the lead?

____ Were you able to probe beyond the surface to get at deeper levels of understanding?

____ What kinds of questions worked best for you?

____ Were you able to encourage the child to elaborate on his or her ideas?

____ What would you have done differently?

____ What specific examples can you find in the transcript about particular moments when you wish you had interacted differently, posed a certain question, or chosen to be silent?

____ What additional questions would you want to ask the child to gain deeper understanding? Again, be very specific.

____ Most important: What have you learned from this project that may help you become a better teacher? What are the practical implications for your classroom of what you learned? What questions have emerged for you as a result of conducting this project?

Reviewer's Summary

What were the main strengths of this paper?

What questions were raised for you as you read the paper?

What specific recommendations do you have for improving the paper? (Please include any items from the checklist, as well as issues regarding specific content ideas, clarity of writing, spelling, grammar, and organization.

Appendix C

An Annotated Bibliography:
Books for Children and Young Adults

The following annotated bibliography contains books that can serve as springboards for discussing themes highlighted in this book. We have included everything from picture books to full-length novels in a variety of genres: poetry, contemporary and historical realism, fantasy, science fiction, folklore, and even nonfiction titles. Some are old favorites and others are newer. We have tried to represent a variety of cultures as well as gender roles for both male and female characters. We believe all the books to be of high literary quality; many have won awards. (Refer to Cullinan & Galda, 1997, for further reference on literature selection.) The books in this bibliography have been chosen for their fit with the themes. Of course, there are many others we might have included. These are only a sample from among our favorites. You will certainly add your own favorite books to the list. Most of the titles could easily fit within several of the categories. The categories are by nature closely interconnected—that is part of what we hope the discussions will demonstrate. Our classification system of P (primary), I (intermediate), and A (advanced) is borrowed from Cullinan and Galda (1997).

STUDENTS' EXPERIENCES OF SCHOOL

Cohen, B. (1983). *Molly's pilgrim.* New York: Dell. ISBN 0-440-41057-6.

Molly has moved with her family from Russia to the United States. Her new classmates ridicule her speech and her clothing. Molly's wise mother helps restore Molly's confidence and gain the understanding of the children at school. (P)

Cohen, M. (1980). *First grade takes a test.* New York: Greenwillow. ISBN 0-688-84265-8.

When the children in this book take their first standardized test, one child is sure she did well, but most are left feeling confused. This brief but insightful little book raises many issues related to assessment and evaluation. (P)

Danzinger, P. (1974). *The cat ate my gymsuit*. New York: Delacorte. ISBN 0-440-01696-7.

Marcie sees herself as "mousy," overweight, and unattractive. Like many teen-age girls, she worries about fitting in, dressing for gym class, and looking pretty. A new English teacher helps Marcie find her voice and learn to value who she is. (A)

dePaola, T. (1989). *The art lesson*. New York: Putnam. ISBN 0-399-21688-X.

Tommy loves to draw and looks forward to first grade when he'll have art lessons in school. However, when the art teacher finally arrives, Tommy is dismayed to find that her concept of art and his own are quite different. (P)

Feiffer, J. (1993). *The man in the ceiling*. New York: HarperCollins. ISBN 0-06-205907-6.

Young Jimmy is a gifted cartoonist who doesn't feel appreciated by his family and who doesn't find school at all interesting. At first, he sees himself through his father's disapproving eyes, but eventually Uncle Charley helps Jimmy to take a different view of who he is and to understand the value of his talent and perspective. (I)

Naidoo, B. (1990). *Chain of fire*. New York: HarperCollins. ISBN 0-397-32426-X.

A group of Black students in a South African high school become part of the resistance to the Apartheid government. There are important contrasts between a friendly, supportive teacher and an intimidating principal who sides against the students. This book can lead to interesting comparisons between its school setting and those in the United States, as well as to more fundamental issues such as the purposes of schooling. (A)

Paterson, K. (1996). *Jip: His story*. New York: Dutton. ISBN 0-525-67543-4.

Abandoned as a young child, Jip grows up on a "poor farm" in Vermont in the mid-1800s. As the most able-bodied and -minded resident, much of the farm's responsibilities fall to Jip, who is taken advantage of by the couple who supervise the farm. Jip convinces his supervisors to allow him to attend school, where he is befriended by a kind teacher who helps him take control of his life. (I)

Paterson, K. (1977). *Bridge to Terabithia*. New York: Harper Collins. ISBN 0-06-440184-7.

Jesse has no close friends at school and feels out of place in his family full of sisters. When Leslie's family moves into the community, she and Jesse become best friends. Their imaginary kingdom of Terabithia becomes a special place in which the two children play and explore together until a tragic accident occurs. The book includes school scenes that highlight Jesse's special relationship with the music teacher as well as ways in which Jesse and Leslie are different from the other kids. (I)

Taylor, M. (1976). *Roll of thunder, hear my cry*. New York: Dial. ISBN 0-803-77473-7.

In the Depression era South, Cassie Logan attends the all-Black school in which her mother teaches. This book raises several issues related to social constructivism, including the startling conditions of the school and Mrs. Logan's resistance to them, the nature of relationships within the Black community and between the Black and White communities, and the understanding Cassie is constructing about racism. (A)

Yashima, T. (1955). *Crow boy*. New York: Penguin. ISBN 0-670-24931-9.

Chibi's first 5 years of school are marked by ridicule and rejection from the other children. Finally, a new teacher takes an interest in Chibi and helps the other children discover what an interesting, talented boy he is. (P)

Additional book titles relating to students' experiences of school:

COMMUNITY AND CLASSROOM CULTURES

Bunting, E. (1991). *Jumping the nail*. Orlando, FL: Harcourt Brace. ISBN 0-152-41357-X.

Dru experiences her first love and worries about her high school friends daring to jump a deep canyon in their efforts to achieve group acceptance. (A)

Bunting, E. (1994). *Smoky night*. San Diego, CA: Harcourt Brace. ISBN 0-152-699541-6.

From his apartment window, Daniel witnesses rioting in the streets of his multi-ethnic neighborhood. In the aftermath of fires, Daniel's family and others seek refuge in a shelter, where Daniel begins to understand racial tensions, and two families begin to bridge their cultural differences. (I)

Byars, B. (1977). *The pinballs*. New York: Scholastic. ISBN 0-590-32427-6.

"One summer two boys and a girl went to a foster home to live together." Thus begins the story of Harvey, Thomas J., and Carley, who find themselves in the foster home of Mr. and Mrs. Mason. Being part of a caring family community is a new experience for these children. As they get to know each other, they get to know themselves as well, and each reaches some sense of resolution about his or her situation. (I)

Curtis, C. P. (1995). *The Watsons go to Birmingham, 1963*. New York: Delacorte. ISBN: 0-385-32175-9.

Nine-year-old Kenny describes life in an African American family in Flint, Michigan and in Birmingham, Alabama during the Civil Rights era. His stories are both funny and poignant. Several chapters include school scenes. (A)

Kendall, C. (1959). *The gammage cup*. New York: Harcourt Brace. ISBN 0-152-30575-0.

This engaging fantasy about the Minnipins, or little people, highlights issues of conformity and individualism within the small community of Slipper-by-the-Sea. The town is ruled by an aristocratic family, the Periods, and everyone is expected to follow the Periods' rules and examples. A small group of outlaw individualists are seen as a threat to the community because they are different. Banished for daring to challenge the status quo, the outlaws thwart an enemy attack and become heroes by saving the town that rejected them. (I)

Lowry, L. (1993). *The giver*. Boston: Houghton Mifflin. ISBN: 0 395-64566-2.

In this gripping science fiction novel for young adults, the concept of community is taken to its extreme. Individuals are completely subordinate to the community, which is strictly governed by a small group of elders. Community members' thoughts, feelings, and relationships are all under the jurisdiction of the elders. (A)

Onyefulu, I. (1996). *Ogbo: Sharing life in an African village*. San Diego, CA: Harcourt Brace. ISBN 0-15-200498-X.

Six-year-old Obioma describes the role of the ogbo, or age group, in contributing to the day-to-day life of her Nigerian village. Each member of the community belongs to an ogbo, and each ogbo has a different function, such as keeping the village clean, cleaning the water source, singing at special events, and building schools. This book, beautifully illustrated with color photographs, provides a rich glimpse into a culture in which the life of the individual depends on the health of the community as a whole. (A)

Paterson, K. (1978). *The great Gilly Hopkins*. New York: HarperCollins. ISBN 0-06-440201-0.

Gilly has been moved from foster home to foster home. She has been hurt deeply by her mother's leaving and has learned to reject other people before they have a chance to reject her. She's a tough cookie at school and often causes trouble for her teachers. Her new foster family, however, changes all that, and Gilly learns what it feels like to be loved and to belong. She even has a new teacher who makes the effort to understand and support her. (I)

Rylant, C. (1982). *When I was young in the mountains*. New York: Dutton. ISBN 0-14-054875-0.

The young narrator fondly describes her Appalachian childhood, offering possibilities for disussion of how we are shaped by place, time, and community. (P)

Soto, G. (1995). *Chato's kitchen*. New York: G. P. Putnam's Sons. ISBN 0-399-22658-3.

Chato (cat) invites his new neighbors, a family of mice, to dinner, intending for them to *be* dinner. When the mice bring their friend Chorizo (a dog) with them, Chato's plans change. Seeing the dog, Chato is initially afraid, but Chorizo's friendliness eases his fears. The story ends with cats, mice, and dog partaking of the delicious meal together, if not becoming friends. (P)

Soto, G. (1992). *Neighborhood odes*. San Diego: Harcourt Brace Jovanovich. ISBN 0-15-256879-4.

Soto's collection of poems depict life in the Mexican American community where he grew up. Poems about the local library, the neighborhood park, a wedding, and even about eating hot tortillas on the lawn have a distinct Hispanic flavor, yet also cross cultural boundaries. Taken as a whole, they provide a rich glimpse into neighborhood life through the eyes of a young boy. (P)

Spinelli, J. (1990). *Maniac Magee*. New York: Harper Collins. ISBN 0-316-80722-2.

Twelve-year-old "Maniac" makes a big impression on Two Mills, Pennsylvania. He is a displaced, homeless boy who manages not only to build a caring community for himself, but to change the dynamics between two rival neighborhoods in Two Mills. (I)

Additional book titles relating to students' experiences of community and classroom:

INQUIRY AS A WAY OF KNOWING

Baylor, B. (1974). *Everybody needs a rock*. New York: Scribner's. ISBN 0-684-13899-9.

The very particular rock owner lays out her 10 rules for selecting the perfect rock as a friend. This simple text can spark conversations about nature study and closer observation of the simplest objects in the world around us. (P)

Baylor, B. (1986). *I'm in charge of celebrations*. New York: Scribner's. ISBN 0-684-18579-2.

The girl narrator shares her observations about the wonders of the desert where she lives. She creates her own special holidays to commemorate moments that have touched her: Rainbow Celebration Day, Green Cloud Day, and Coyote Day. The joys of careful observation of the natural world is a strong theme. (I)

Cleaver, V., & Cleaver, B. (1969). *Where the lilies bloom*. Philadelphia: J. P. Lippincott. ISBN 0-397-31111-7.

A family of children learn how to survive on their own in the mountains after the deaths of both parents; wildcrafting, earning a living, keeping it all a secret. (A)

Cushman, K. (1995). *The midwife's apprentice*. New York: Clarion. ISBN 0-395-69229-6.

Brat, as she is known at the beginning of the story, is homeless, hungry, alone, and is often the target of cruel treatment by townspeople. She becomes apprentice to the village midwife, takes the name of Alyce, and discovers a meaningful place for herself in the world. Alyce's powerful motivations for learning about midwifery and folk medicine, as well as how to read, are driven by her need to belong and to connect with other people. She learns about things relevant to her needs through observing, trying things out for herself, and refining her theories as she works. (A)

DeFelice, C. (1996). *The apprenticeship of Lucas Whitaker*. New York: Farrar Straus Giroux. ISBN 0-374-34669-0.

Orphaned by the consumption that has wiped out his community, young Lucas makes his way to a new town where he apprentices himself to the doctor. Lucas sets about learning everything he can from the doctor by observing, listening, and trying his own hand at making folks better. His motivations are all the stronger because he wants to discover how to relieve the sickness that destroyed his family. (I)

Paulsen, G. (1987). *Hatchet*. New York: Bradbury. ISBN 0-027-70130-1.

Stranded alone in the Canadian woods, Brian Robseon learns how to survive on his own by studying his environment and becoming a careful observer of nature. (A)

Pinkney, A. D. (1996). *Bill Pickett: Rodeo ridin' cowboy*. San Diego: Harcourt Brace. ISBN 0-15-200100-X.

This biography of the noted African-American cowboy describes Bill's boyhood fascination with the cowboys who herded cattle past his family's farm. His observations of the cowboys and of the cattle themselves led him to invent a technique for "bulldogging," or wrestling steers, and to become legendary for his accomplishments. (P)

Pinkney, B. (1995). *JoJo's flying side kick*. New York: Simon & Schuster. ISBN 0-689-80283-8.

JoJo is anxious about the test for her yellow belt in Tae Kwon Do. She seeks assistance from members of her family, who teach her their own techniques for learning and refining a new skill. Finally, JoJo passes the test by inventing her own technique based on the ones she's learned about from her family. (P)

Yolen, J. (1987). *Owl moon*. New York: Philomel. ISBN 0-399-21457-7.

This brief, elegant story provides opportunities for thinking about how we learn in the world outside of school. A father and child go owling on a winter night and notice many subtleties of the woods where they walk. (P)

Additional book titles relating to inquiry and ways of knowing:

CONSIDERATION OF MULTIPLE PERSPECTIVES

Asch, F., & Vagin, V. (1989). *Here comes the cat!* New York: Scholastic. ISBN 0-590-41854-8.

Word spreads among the mice across the countryside and into the town, "Here comes the cat!" As the cat approaches, and his shadow looms large, a surprise awaits readers with traditional views of cat and mouse relationships. (P)

Avi. (1991). *Nothing but the truth*. New York: Avon. ISBN 0-380-71907-X.

Philip Malloy does not like his English teacher, Miss Narwin. To annoy her, he hums the national anthem as it is played over the loudspeaker in Miss Narwin's homeroom class—*almost* breaking the rule against singing. He challenges Miss Narwin's caution about the rule. One thing leads to another, and Philip Malloy finds himself the center of a raging political and media debate about freedom of speech. The novel is written as a "documentary," through a series of memos, diary entries, letters, and scripts. Readers have access to the perspectives of Philip, other students, his parents, Miss Narwin, administrators, and others. (A)

Carrick, C. (1986). *What happened to Patrick's dinosaurs?* New York: Clarion. ISBN 0-89919-797-3.

Patrick describes to his older brother Hank his conception of what dinosaurs must have been like. As Patrick talks, Hank poses questions to scaffold Patrick's elaboration on his theories about dinosaurs. This book can serve as a fun "model" for eliciting and appreciating children's perspectives. (P)

Dorris, M. (1992). *Morning Girl*. New York: Hyperion. ISBN 1-562-82284-5.

Morning Girl and her brother Star Boy present their two perspectives as they narrate alternate chapters in this brief book. The story depicts Native American perspectives on family, our relationship to the earth, and the arrival of the Europeans in the New World. (I)

Dorris, M. (1994). *Guests*. New York: Hyperion. ISBN 0-7868-0047-X.

Moss does not understand why his father has invited strangers to participate in his village's harvest feast. In search of answers, Moss goes into the forest for time alone to learn about himself and the kind of man he is to become. This short novel about the first Thanksgiving is presented from the perspective of a young Native American boy who is a reluctant host to those early guests. (I)

Esbensen, B. J. (1992). *Who shrank my grandmother's house? Poems of discovery*. New York: Harper Collins. ISBN 0-060-21828-2.

Esbensen's "poems of discovery" nudge readers to see mundane objects and events with new eyes. Poems focus on such everyday topics as a napping cat, a door, and a rain storm. (P–I)

Farber, N. (1979). *How does it feel to be old?* New York: Dutton. ISBN 0-525-32414-3.

This child's question of her grandmother prompts a wonderful stream of memories. In her poetic answer, the grandmother describes her perspective to the child, including both the joys and the challenges of being old. (P)

Glenn, M. (1996). *Who killed Mr. Chippendale? A mystery in poems*. New York: Dutton. ISBN 0-525-67530-2.

In this novel written as a series of poems, various members of the high school community speak about the murder of teacher Mr. Chippendale. Readers hear from students, guidance counselor, principal, and others about the kind of teacher Mr. Chippendale had been, what it was like to be in his classroom, and who might have wanted to hurt him. Along the way clues are provided as to the identity and motive of the murderer, and the mystery is finally solved. (A)

MacLachlan, P. (1991). *Journey*. New York: Dell. ISBN 0-440-40809-1.

When Journey's mother leaves him and his sister with their grandparents yet again, Journey feels abandoned and unwanted. His warm, understanding grandparents support him as he tries to understand his mother and why she left. Through photography, which he learns from his grandfather, Journey discovers the value in seeing from different points of view and finds contentment in his situation. (I)

Martin, R. (1989). *Will's mammoth*. New York: Putnam. ISBN 0-399-21627-8.

This story of few words is a delightful romp through Will's fantasy world in which woolly mammoths are his playmates. Only Will, and not his parents, can see the mammoths. (P)

Mochizuki, K. (1995). *Heroes*. New York: Lee & Low. ISBN 1-880-00050-4.

This touching story shares the perspective of Donnie, a Japanese American child in the aftermath of World War II. His classmates treat him differently, always casting him in the role of "enemy" in their war games. When his reserved and dignified father and uncle finally show Donnie's playmates that they fought for the United States in the war, the children recognize their prejudice and see Donnie and his family in a new light. (P)

Monfried, L. (1990). *The daddies boat* New York: Penguin. ISBN 0-525-44584-6.

The little girl narrator describes all the things she does during the week on her Northeastern island home as she waits for the "daddies boat" each Friday, that brings all the commuting daddies back from their work on the mainland. The surprise ending reveals why she finds "daddies boat" a silly nickname. (P)

Van Allsburg, C. (1993). *The sweetest fig*. Boston: Houghton Mifflin. ISBN 0-395-67346-1.

Monsieur Bibot, an ill-natured dentist, receives payment of two magical figs from a patient. Marcel, his mistreated dog, eats one and changes places with his owner. Readers are left to imagine how Bibot, now a dog, might see the world very differently. (P)

Whiteley, O. (1994). *Only Opal: The diary of a young girl*. New York: Putnam. ISBN 0-399-21990-0.

This picture book is drawn from the diary of Opal Whiteley, an orphan who was adopted by a pioneer couple and used as a laborer. Opal's diary entries reveal her innocent, childlike perspective, which stands in stark contrast to that of her adoptive parents. (I)

Yolen, J. (1992). *Encounter.* San Diego: Harcourt Brace Jovanovich. ISBN 0-152-25962-7.

This story of the arrival of Columbus in the New World is narrated by a young Taino boy. The perspective on Columbus is, naturally, quite different from the way he has been portrayed in most social studies textbooks. An interesting aspect of the story to which children often respond is that the boy senses something ominous about Columbus and warns the adults around him, but his warnings are dismissed because he is but a child. (I)

Young, E. (1992). *Seven blind mice.* New York: Scholastic. ISBN 0-590-46971-1.

This retelling of the Indian tale of "The Blind Men and the Elephant" casts mice as the characters. Each mouse feels a different part of the elephant's body and, unable to see the whole creature, mistakenly assumes that the part *is* the whole. It is only after the mice combine their perspectives that they are able to identify the elephant as an elephant. (P)

Additional book titles relating to consideration of multiple perspectives:

MOTIVATION AND SENSE OF AGENCY

Avi. (1994). *The barn.* New York: Orchard. ISBN 0-531-06861-7.

Ben's father has fallen ill, and Ben—the youngest of three—leads his siblings in caring for their father and honoring his last wish of building a new barn on the Oregon Territory homestead. (A)

Babbit, N. (1987). *Tuck everlasting.* New York: Dell. ISBN 0-440-84095-3.

Winnie, who has been sheltered from the world beyond her front gate, feels powerless to change her life. When she becomes involved with the Tuck family, however, her outlook changes, and Winnie finds powerful motivation for taking control of her life and helping the Tucks. (I)

Cumming, P. (1986). *C.L.O.U.D.S.* New York: Lothrop, Lee & Shepard. ISBN 0-688-04682-7.

Chuku is discouraged when he receives his first assignment as a cloud designer for New York City. The sky there is boring, and no one ever looks up to notice it anyway. He is stifled by the restrictive rules for designing clouds. At the risk of reprisal from his supervisor, Chuku designs beautiful, many-colored sky scenes for New York and eventually breaks a cardinal rule of cloud design in order to make contact with one little girl who always notices his handiwork. Children who feel they are always being "bossed around" may identify with Chuku and his need to take matters into his own hands. (P)

Cushman, K. (1994). *Catherine, called Birdy.* New York: Clarion. ISBN 0-395-68186-3.

Not wanting to fall in line with her parents' and society's expectations, Birdy resists the role being thrust upon her in this novel of the Middle Ages. Worried about the impending marriage her father is trying to arrange, Birdy takes action to thwart each suitor brought to the manor. Unlike the image of the damsel in distress, Birdy takes an active role in shaping her life as she chooses. (A)

Konigsburg, E. L. (1967). *From the mixed-up files of Mrs. Basil E. Frankwieler.* New York: Atheneum. ISBN 0-689-70308-2.

Claudia is one child who knows she has the power to bring about change on her own behalf. Feeling unappreciated, she forms and executes elaborate plans for running away from home and hiding in the Metropolitan Museum of Art. Along the way, she undertakes an inquiry into the life and art of Michelangelo because she feels a strong connection to a statue rumored to have been created by the famous artist. (I)

Lasky, K. (1995). *She's wearing a dead bird on her head!* New York: Hyperion. ISBN 0-786-80065-8.

Believing the fashion of having stuffed birds mounted on women's hats to be inhumane, two women set out to change society's views about the relations between people and animals. Not only do they succeed in getting legislation passed, but they also found the Audubon Society. (P)

Levine, A. A. (1993). *Pearl Moscowitz's last stand.* New York: William Morrow. ISBN 0-688-10754-0.

Pearl and a group of women friends in her multi-ethnic inner-city community become activists when the city threatens to take down the last Gingko tree on their street. Ultimately, the women win and save the tree, revitalizing the community spirit of the neighborhood in the process. (P)

Naylor, P.R. (1991). *Shiloh*. New York: Atheneum. ISBN 0-689-31614-3.

Marty goes to great effort to save an abused hunting dog from its owner's malicious treatment. Motivated by his intense empathy and love for the dog, Shiloh, Marty goes against his parents' wishes, risks punishment, and struggles within himself as he decides whether deceiving his parents, friends, and the dog's owner is justified. (I)

Rosen, M. J. (1995). *A school for Pompey Walker*. San Diego: Harcourt Brace. ISBN 0-15-200114-X.

Pompey Walker, an ex-slave, conspires with a White man to be sold into slavery again and again, only to escape and repeat the scam. The money the two men raise is used to build a school for Black children. Pompey's motivation comes from his own childhood dreams of attending school and learning to read and write. (I)

Additional book titles relating to motivation and sense of agency:

THEORIES OF KNOWLEDGE

Dickinson, P. (1988). *Eva*. New York: Dell. ISBN 0-440-207660-5.

Following a tragic automobile accident, Eva wakes up from a coma to discover that her body has been destroyed. Thanks to technological developments, her neuron memory (the pattern in the brain that constituted her identity) has been transferred to the body of a chimp. Eva's consciousness and memories are alive inside the chimp body. This story of Eva's shift from shock to acceptance of her new circumstances raises issues of identity (what makes us *us*?) and knowledge (how do we come to know?). (A)

Lowry, L. (1979). *Anastasia Krupnik*. New York: Dell. ISBN 0-440-40852-0.

Ten-year-old Anastasia is encountering many new freelings and experiences. Her parents are expecting a baby, her grandmother can't remember

Anastasia's name, her teacher doesn't understand her, and the boy on whom she has a crush doesn't know she exists. Anastasia uses her private notebook to sort out her feelings about all these issues and more, learning a great deal about herself in the process. (I)

Sis, P. (1996). *Starry messenger: A book depicting the life of a famous scientist, mathematician, astronomer, philosopher, physicist, Galileo Galilei.* New York: Farrar Straus Giroux. ISBN 0-374-37191-1.

Galileo made many discoveries about the universe and the earth's place in it. Because of some of his new knowledge, he was tried by the Pope's court and sentenced to spend the rest of his life locked in his own house. Still, he refused to deny what he knew to be true and continued to share his ideas whenever he could. (I)

Stanley, D. (1996). *Leonardo da Vinci.* New York: Morrow. ISBN 0-688-10437-1.

Leonardo da Vinci was truly a knower. He was interested in a wide array of knowledge, from art to astronomy, biology, and beyond. His ideas were sometimes far ahead of his time and were often challenged or doubted. (I)

Staples, S. F. (1996). *Dangerous skies.* New York: Farrar Straus Giroux. ISBN 0-374-31694-5.

Buck knows in his heart that his best friend Tunes did not commit the crime of which she is accused. He despairs when even his own father doubts his word, yet Buck clings to the truth he knows. (A)

Additional book titles relating to theories of knowledge:

Glossary

Behaviorism—A theory of learning, based on the work of pioneers such as John B. Watson and B. F. Skinner that emphasizes operant, or instrumental conditioning, and focuses on controlling actions through reinforcement of specific behaviors.

Children's thinking project—A project we have designed for the purposes of promoting understanding of social constructivist theory and of various ways to gain better access to children's construction of meaning. The project involves conducting and taping a conversation with a student and analyzing the processes and the content of that conversation, emphasizing self-critique.

Classroom culture—The set of socially constructed understandings regarding concerns such as roles, rules, relationships, values, and notions of authority in a classroom.

Coding—A process used in data analysis in which one identifies, sorts out, and names key topics or patterns that are found in data. Similar to creating an index or filing system for ideas that enables a researcher to identify and organize the findings of an inquiry. Codes are generated according to the particular focus of the inquiry. They might include, for example, participants' perspectives about a certain topic, processes over time, activities, events, or relationships among people.

Concept map–mind map—A visual representation illustrating the relationships among key ideas or concepts that can be helpful in constructing and expanding holistic understanding.

Continuing impulse to learn (CIL)—A form of intrinsic motivation based on the social constructivist view in which engagement in learning is propelled and focused by thought and feeling emerging from a learner's processes of constructing meaning. CIL is characterized by intense involvement, curiosity, and a search for understanding, where learners experience learning as a deeply personal and continuing agenda.

Democratic education—Education that critiques existing political and social systems to prepare learners to take action for bringing about social change. Democratic education encompasses both the content and processes of education.

Ebonics—A term coined by Robert L. Williams in 1973 that refers to language of Caribbean, and U.S. slave descendants of West African origins. Accepted by many linguists as an African language system, because it retains the Niger–Congo grammar system, but employs many English words.

Epistemology—A theory of knowledge, of how we come to know, of our ways of knowing. Social constructivism is one example of an epistemological theory.

Intrinsic motivation—Motivation that a person experiences as being based on inherent interest or value of a particular activity, rather than as a result of extrinsic purposes or rewards not related to the activity.

Inquiry-based learning—An approach to curriculum that places students' questions at the center and uses the disciplines as lenses for exploring those questions. Students take on the roles of scientists, writers, artists, historians, mathematicians, and so forth, applying appropriate tools and skills that are part of curricular requirements, as they seek to answer their questions.

Learning autobiography—A written personal history focused on an individual's own experiences as a learner, highlighting important themes or core issues.

More knowledgeable other—A Vygotskian concept that identifies a person who interacts with a learner in ways that promote the learner's understanding.

Optimal challenge level—The level of challenge at which an individual is neither bored (from lack of challenge) or overwhelmed (through too difficult a challenge), and that, therefore, supports learning and motivation most effectively.

Scaffold—A process, defined by Wood, Bruner, and Ross, through which a more knowledgeable other facilitates a learner's knowledge construction.

Social constructivism—A theory of knowledge that holds that knowledge is constructed within a social context through language and other sign systems. A social constructivist perspective focuses on learning as sense-making and not on the acquisition of knowledge that "exists" somewhere outside the learner.

Understandings—A term used to describe the multiple constructions of reality that are part of social constructivist theory.

References

Allen, J. B. (Ed.). (1999). *Class actions: Teaching for social justice in elementary and middle school.* New York: Teachers College Press.

Allen, J., Delgado, L., & Cary, M. (Eds.). (1995). *Exploring blue highways: Literacy reform, school change, and the creation of learning communities.* New York: Teachers College Press.

Alvermann, D. E. (1991). The discussion web: A graphic aid for learning across the curriculum. *The Reading Teacher, 45*(2), 92–99.

Barr, M. A., & Syverson, M. A. (1994). *California learning record: A handbook for teachers, K–6.* San Diego, CA: University of California at San Diego Bookstore.

Barrs, M., Ellis, S., Hester, H., & Thomas, A. (1989). *Primary language record.* Portsmouth, NH: Heinemann.

Cobb, P., Yackel, E., & Wood, T. (1992). Interaction and learning in mathematics classroom situations. *Educational Studies in Mathematics, 23,* 99–122.

Cohen, M. (1980). *First grade takes a test.* New York: Greenwillow.

Calkins, L. M. (1994). *The art of teaching writing.* Portsmouth, NH: Heinemann.

Commeyras, M. (1995). What can we learn from students' questions? *Theory Into Practice, 34*(2), 101–106.

Covington, M. V. (1985). The motive for self-worth. In C. Ames & R. Ames (Eds.), *Research on motivation in education: The classroom milieu* (pp. 77–113). San Diego, CA: Academic Press.

Cross, C. (1990). National goals: Four priorities for educational researchers. *Educational Researcher, 19*(8), 21–24.

Csikszentmihalyi, M. (1978). Intrinsic rewards and emergent motivation. In M. Lepper & D. Greene (Eds.), *The hidden cost of reward: New perspectives on the psychology of human motivation* (pp. 205–216). Hillsdale, NJ: Erlbaum.

Cullinan, B. E., & Galda, L. (1997). *Literature and the child.* Ft. Worth, TX: Harcourt Brace.

Dahl, K. L., & Freppon, P. A. (1995). A comparison of inner-city children's interpretations of reading and writing instruction in the early grades in skills-based and whole language classrooms. *Reading Research Quarterly, 30*(1), 50–74.

Daniels, H. (1994). *Literature circles: Voice and choice in the student-centered classroom.* York, ME: Stenhouse.

Deci, E. L., & Ryan, R. (1987). *Intrinsic motivation and self-determination in human behavior.* New York: Plenum Press.

Deci, E. L., & Ryan, R. M. (1990). A motivational approach to self: Integration in personality. In D. Dienstbier (Ed.), *Nebraska Symposium on Motivation* (pp. 237–288). Lincoln, NE: University of Nebraska Press.

Delpit, L. (1997). What should teachers do? Ebonics and culturally responsive instruction. In Perry, T. & Delpit, L. (Eds.). (1997). The real ebonics debate: Power, language and the education of African-American children [Special issue]. *Rethinking Schools: An Urban Educational Journal, 13*(1), 6–7.

Dewey, J. (1928, March). *Progressive education and the science of education.* Paper presented at the eighth annual conference of the Progressive Education Association, Washington, DC.

Duckworth, E. (1987). *"The having of wonderful ideas" and other essays on teaching and learning.* New York: Teachers College Press.

Dyson, A. H. (1989). *Multiple worlds of child writers: Friends learning to write.* New York: Teachers College Press.

Dyson, A. H. (1991). The word and the world: Reconceptualizing written language development, or, Do rainbows mean a lot to little girls? *Research in the Teaching of English, 25,* 97–123.

Edelsky, C. (1994). Education for democracy. *Language Arts, 71,* 252–257.

Feiffer, J. (1993). *The man in the ceiling.* San Antonio, TX: HarperCollins.

Fosnot, C. T. (1996). Constructivism: A psychological theory of learning. In C. T. Fosnot (Ed.), *Constructivism: theory, perspectives and practice* (pp. 8–33). New York. Teachers College Press.

George, J. C. (1972). *Julie of the wolves.* New York: Trumpet.

Getridge, C. (1997). Oakland superintendent responds to critics of the ebonics policy. *Rethinking Schools, 12*(1), 27.

Glenn, M. (1996). *Who killed Mr. Chippendale? A mystery in poems.* New York: Dutton.

Goodman, J. (1989). Education for critical democracy. *Journal of Education, 171*(2), 88–116.

Goodman, J. (1992). *Elementary schooling for critical democracy.* Albany, NY: State University of New York Press.

Goodman, Y. M. (1989). Evaluation of students: Evaluation of teachers. In K. S. Goodman, Y. M. Goodman, & W. J. Hood (Eds.), *The whole language evaluation book* (pp. 3–14). Portsmouth, NH: Heinemann.

Goodman, Y. M., & Goodman, K. S. (1990). Vygotsky in a whole language perspective. In L. C. Moll (Ed.), *Vygotsky and education: Instructional implications and applications of sociohistorical psychology* (pp. 223–250). New York: Cambridge University Press.

Green, J., & Dixon, C. (1996). Language of literacy dialogues: Facing the future or reproducing the past. *Journal of Literacy Research, 28*(2), 289–301.

Greene, M. (1995). *Releasing the imagination: Essays on education, the arts, and social change.* San Francisco: Jossey-Bass.

Guba, E. G., & Lincoln, Y. S. (1989). *Fourth generation evaluation.* Newbury Park, CA: Sage.

Hankins, K. H. (1996). One moment in two times. *Teacher Research: The Journal of Classroom Inquiry, 4*(1), 24–28.

Harste, J., Short, K., & Burke, C. (1995). *Creating classrooms for authors and inquirers.* Portsmouth, NH: Heinemann.

Heath, S. B. (1983). *Ways with words: Language, life and work in communities and classrooms.* New York: Holt, Rinehart & Winston.

Heshusius, L. (1995). Listening to children: "What could we possibly have in common?" From concerns with self to participatory consciousness. *Theory Into Practice, 34*(2), 117–123.

Huck, C. S. (1990). The power of children's literature in the classroom. In K. G. Short & K. M. Pierce (Eds.), *Talking about books: Creating literate communities* (pp. 3–15). Portsmouth, NH: Heinemann.

Hutchins, P. (1968). *Rosie's walk.* New York: Aladdin.

Kagan, S. (1997). *Cooperative learning.* Laguna Beach, CA: Kagan Cooperative Publishers.

Kelly, G. J., & Green, J. (1998). The social nature of knowing: Toward a sociocultural perspective on conceptual change and knowledge construction. In B. Guzzetti & C. Hynd (Eds.), *Perspectives on conceptual change.* Mahwah, NJ: Erlbaum.

Kohn, A. (1993). *Punished by rewards: The trouble with gold stars, incentive plans, A's, praise, and other bribes.* Boston: Houghton Mifflin.

Kuzmic, J. (1993). Community, voice, and democratic schooling: Curriculum possibilities in an age of individualism. *Curriculum and Teaching, 8*(1), 39–56.

Lampkins, M. (1997). An Oakland student speaks out. *Rethinking Schools, 12*(1), 29.

Linguistic Society of America. (1997). Resolution on ebonics. *Rethinking Schools, 12*(1), 27.

Lyons, N. (1990). Dilemmas of knowing: Ethical and epistemological dimensions of teachers' work and development. *Harvard Educational Review, 60*(2) 159–180.

Marshall, H. H. (1992). *Redefining student learning: Roots of educational change.* Norwood, NJ: Ablex.

McCombs, B. L. (1991). Motivation and lifelong learning. *Educational Psychologist, 26*(2), 117–127.

McCombs, B. L., & Marzano, R. J. (1990). Putting the self in self-regulated learning: The self as agent in integrating will and skills. *Educational Psychologist, 25*(1), 51–69.

Moll, L. C., & Gonzalez, N. (1994). Lessons from research with language-minority children. *Journal of Reading Behavior, 26*(4), 439–456.

Nicholls, J. G. (1989). *The competitive ethos and democratic education.* Cambridge, MA: Harvard University Press.

Nicholls, J. G., & Hazzard, S. P. (1993). *Education as adventure: Lessons from the second grade.* New York: Teachers College Press.

O'Flahavan, J., Gambrell, L. B., Guthrie, J., Stahl, S., Baumann, J. S., & Alvermann, D. E. (1992, *August/September*). Poll of IRA members guides national reading research center. *Reading Today*, p. 12.

Oldfather, P. (1992, December). *Sharing the ownership of knowing: A constructivist concept of motivation for literacy learning.* Paper presented at the annual meeting of the National Reading Conference, San Antonio, TX.

Oldfather, P. (1993). What students say about motivating experiences in a whole language classroom. *The Reading Teacher, 46*(8), 672–681.

Oldfather, P., Bonds, S., & Bray, T. (1994). Stalking the fuzzy sunshine seeds: Constructivist processes for teaching about constructivism in teacher education. *Teacher Education Quarterly, 21*(3), 5–14.

Oldfather, P., & Dahl, K. (1994). Toward a social constructivist reconceptualization of intrinsic motivation for literacy learning. *JRB: A Journal of Literacy, 28*(2), 139–158.

Oldfather, P., & McLaughlin, J. L. (1993). Gaining and losing voice: A longitudinal study of students' continuing impulse to learn across elementary and middle level contexts. *Research in Middle Level Education, 17*(1), 1–25.

Oldfather, P., & Thomas, S. (1998). What does it mean when teachers participate in collaborative research with high school students on literacy motivations? *Teachers College Record, 90*(4), 647–691.

Oldfather, P., & Thomas, S. (in press). "The changer and the changed": The nature and outcomes of students' longitudinal participatory research on literacy motivations and schooling. *Research in the Teaching of English.*

Paris, S. G., & Ayers, L. R. (1994). *Becoming reflective students and teachers with portfolios and authentic assessment.* Washington, DC: American Psychological Assocation.

Perry, T. (1997). Reflections on the Ebonics debate: "'I 'on know why they be trippin.'" In Perry, T., & Delpit. L. (Eds.). (1997). The real ebonics debate: Power, language and the education of African-American children [Special issue]. *Rethinking Schools: An Urban Educational Journal, 13*(1).

Piaget, J. (1955). *The language and thought of the child.* New York: New American Library.

Popp, M. S. (1997). *Learning journals in the K–8 classroom: Exploring ideas and information in the content areas.* Mahwah, NJ: Erlbaum.

Portalupi, J. (1995). Autobiographical understanding: Writing the past into the future. *Language Arts, 72,* 272–274.

Shannon, P. (1993). Developing democratic voices. *The Reading Teacher, 47*(2), 86–94.

Short, K. G., & Burke, C. (1991). *Creating curriculum: Teachers and students as a community of learners.* Portsmouth, NH: Heinemann.

Short, K. G., & Pierce, K. M. (1990). *Talking about books: Creating literature communities.* Portsmouth, NH: Heinemann.

Skinner, B. F. (1974). *About behaviorism.* New York: Knopf.

Smith, K. (1990). Entertaining a text: A reciprocal process. In K. G. Short & K. M. Pierce (Eds.), *Talking about books: Creating literate communities* (pp. 17–31). Portsmouth, NH: Heinemann.

Strike, K. A., & Posner, G. J. (1992). A revisionist theory of conceptual change. In R. Duschl & R. Hamilton (Eds.), *Philosophy of science, cognitive psychology, and educational theory and practice* (pp. 147–176). Albany, NY: SUNY Press.

Taylor, R. (1982, March). "Meeting the needs of gifted children in the regular classroom." Workshop presentation to the Sioux Falls School District 49–5. Sioux Falls, South Dakota.

Thomas, S. (1994). *Knowing learners—Knowing ourselves: Teachers' perceptions of change in theory and practices resulting from inquiry into authentic assessment.* Unpublished doctoral dissertation, The Claremont Graduate School, Claremont, CA.

Thomas, S., & Oldfather, P. (1995). Enhancing student and teacher engagement in literacy learning: A shared inquiry approach. *The Reading Teacher, 49*(3), 192–202.

Thomas, S., & Oldfather, P. (1997). Intrinsic motivations, literacy, and assessment practices: "That's my grade. That's me." *Educational Psychologist, 32*(2) 107–123.

Vygotsky, L. S. (1978). *Mind in society: The development of higher psychological processes.* Cambridge, MA: Harvard University Press.

Ward, H. (1996). Kids on the move for research: Fifth graders' experience with action research. *Teacher Research: The Journal of Classroom Inquiry, 4*(1), 63–68.

Wardhaugh, R. (1990). *An introduction to sociolinguistics.* Cambridge, MA: Basil Blackwell.

Weade, G. (1992). Locating learning in the times and spaces of teaching. In H. Marshall (Ed.), *Redefining student learning: Roots of educational change* (pp. 87–118). Norwood, NJ: Ablex.

West, J. (1996a, December). *"Are you gonna put a grade on this?" The influence of grades on children's collaboration in literacy learning.* Paper presented at the National Reading Conference, Charleston, SC.

West, J., Wilmarth, J., Crumley, C., Dickerson, J., & Francis, M. (1999). Being social scientists: A democratic experience in teacher education. In Allen, J. (Ed.), *Class actions: Teaching for social justice in elementary and middle school* (pp. 44–58). New York: Teachers College Press.

West, J. (1996b). Getting help when you need it: The relations between social status and third graders' helping interactions during literacy events. In D. J. Leu, C. K. Kinzer, & K. A. Hinchman (Eds.), *Literacies for the 21st century: Research and practice* (pp. 59–75). Chicago, IL: National Reading Conference.

White, R. (1959). Motivation reconsidered: The concept of competence. *Psychology Review, 66,* 297–333.

Whitin, P. (1996). *Sketching stories, stretching minds: Responding visually to literature.* Portsmouth, NH: Heinemann.

Willis, A. I. (1987, April). *Dissin' and Disremembering: Motivation for literacy in schooling.* Paper presented at the annual meeting of the American Educational Research Association, Chicago, IL.

Wood, D., Bruner, J. S., & Ross, B. (1976). The role of tutoring in problem solving. *Journal of Child Psychology and Psychiatry, 17,* 89–100.

Wood, D., & Wood, A. (1984). *The little mouse, the red ripe strawberry, and the big hungry bear.* New York: Scholastic.

ABOUT THE AUTHORS

Penny Oldfather is an associate professor of elementary education at The University of Georgia. She has 16 years of public school experience in teaching and administration. A principal investigator with the National Reading Research Center (1991–1996), Professor Oldfather focuses on student motivation and social constructivism in teaching and learning. She employs qualitative research methods to explore students' perspectives and collaborates with students in participatory action research. Dr. Oldfather has published in such journals as *Educational Researcher, Educational Psychologist, Teachers College Record, Qualitative Inquiry, Journal of Reading Behavior* and *The Reading Teacher.* She has recently served as an associate editor of the *Journal of Literacy Research.*

Jane West is an assistant professor of education at Agnes Scott College. Previously, she taught in elementary and middle school settings, and is currently teaching courses in children's literature, language, literacy, and teacher research. Her courses are inquiry-based and highlight issues of education for democracy. Dr. West's research on children's peer helping during literacy events takes a social constructivist stance and focuses on the perspectives of children in classrooms. She has published in journals such as *Educational Researcher, Qualitative Inquiry, Language Arts,* and *The New Advocate.*

Jennifer White is the Principal of North Jackson Elementary School in Jackson County, Georgia. She holds a master's degree in Language Education and an educational specialist degree in Educational Leadership. She has taught both fourth grade and kindergarten in her rural district. Jennifer works with teachers on instructional issues. Her goal as an administrator is to help the teachers on her faculty see their classrooms through their students' eyes and create inviting classrooms where all students want to be. She has participated in a group of teacher researchers for the last 8 years and has contributed chapters to *Exploring Blue Highways* (edited by Allen, Cary, & Delgado, 1995).

Jill Wilmarth is an upper elementary teacher in Roswell, Georgia. She previously taught fourth and fifth grade in a public school in the Atlanta area. She is a graduate of Agnes Scott College, where her focus was on early childhood education and religious studies. She has co-authored a book chapter (West, Wilmarth, Crumley, Dickerson & Francis, 1999) with some of her college classmates on democratic classroom practices. She has pursued research applying a critical lens to students' perspectives on their learning.